I0374812

First published in Great Britain

2022 by Jack Soley

This publication is the second edition published in 2025.

Copyright © Jack Soley, 2022

Jack Soley has asserted his moral right to be identified as the Author of this work in accordance with the Copyright Designs and Patents Act 1988.

All rights reserved. No part of this publication may be reproduced, stored in a retrieval system, or transmitted in any form or by any means, electronic, mechanical, photocopying, recording or otherwise, without the prior permission of the publisher.

A catalogue record for this book is available from the British Library.

All opinions are of that of the author and do not represent the views of the publishing company or their affiliates.

This book is published by Pomerak Ventures Ltd, registered in England & Wales under the company number 15578139.

ISBN: 9781917706001

Contents

Prologue 6
Essential Equipment 13
   Starter Boards 14
   Buying New or Secondhand 16
   Importing Sandboards from Abroad 20
   Using a Snowboard on Sand 26
   Goggles 30
   Helmets 33
   Pads 36
   Bags 37
   Waxes 39
   Cameras 41
How to be a Sandboarder 45
   Performing Tricks 48
   Speed and Direction Control 50
   Preparing yourself physically 51
   Building Leg Muscles 53
   Stamina 53

    Diet 54

    Water Consumption 55

    Sleep 55

    Aerodynamics (Shaving Legs) 57

    Mindset 58

    Persistence 58

Sandboarding Knowledge and Understanding 61

    What is Sandboarding? 62

    When was Sandboarding invented? 62

    The Etymology of Sandboarding 66

    Is there a competitive element to Sandboarding? 67

    Globalisation of the Sport 67

Issues Facing Sandboarding Today 70

    You Can't Buy Equipment 71

    There aren't many good places for Sandboarding 72

    Demand for Sandboarding is Low 73

    There's not a lot of Events 75

    It's hard to get Insurance 76

    Sandboarding Deaths 78

Interviews With Sandboarders 81

- Alex Bird 81
- Vitor Semedo 84
- Lon Beale 86
- Gabriel Cruz 89
- Jamie Perkins 92

Best Places For Sandboarding 96
- North America 97
- South America 105
- Europe 114
- Asia 123
- Africa 132
- Oceania 142

Sandboarding Bites 153
Final Thoughts 158
References 161

Prologue

During the summer of 2007, I was a bored young lad, and my grandfather came up with the idea of getting a bin lid and going down the dunes at a nearby beach. Still, as it turned out, you could buy round boards created for that sole purpose on that beach, and I remember the first time I went down a dune on a board, I thought that I wanted to carry on, and I couldn't get bored of it! After that, every year I visited my grandparents, I'd always begged to visit Holywell Bay; that was my sanctuary, my abode, that was where my passion began.

After I left school in 2014, I was reluctant to attend college as I had a few fears with being there: it was a new experience, my time in school, which I had just spent around 12 years in, was complete, and I didn't want to be in such a crowded atmosphere with people whom I've never seen; after the first couple of days, it just felt like I was back at school again but with a lot more freedom than what I was used to having.

A month of being in college, I was not speaking to anyone, not knowing anyone, having any enjoyment, or any willingness to be there. So I had an idea to generate a new hobby to be less bored and do something with my spare time. This new hobby of mine had to be something I could commit to, not give up on, and have the potential to inspire other people whilst I was doing it; that hobby turned out to be blogging.

Once I started my blog, the genuine hurdle was what this future blog could be about; as I was studying Business, Finance, and World Development, this didn't help me whatsoever, so I had to think outside the box.

The subject on which my blog would focus was a struggle. I had to choose something interesting, something people would understand, and something that isn't a complex concept. I came up with "Sandboarding". If you're not familiar with Sandboarding, then you shouldn't worry because I've had to endure the pain of everyone around me asking me the same question since I started the blog.

"What's Sandboarding?" and I always give the short but simple response that somehow is the same every time, "Snowboarding on Sand".

I chose Sandboarding because I've been familiar with it for years, and growing up, every time I went to Cornwall on holiday to visit my grandparents. I've always begged to go to Holywell Bay which has a range of dunes; this is why Sandboarding became my blog subject of choice as it's the only sport I've done and one that I know about or even been slightly passionate about doing. I'm not an athlete, and growing up; I haven't been vaguely interested in many pursuits; this happened to be one of them.

"Holywell Bay Sandboarding, Aged 14" from Jack Soley. All Rights Reserved.

It's also worth mentioning that I dropped out of my World Development class on the second day I started college; I failed Finance because I ended up in the wrong exam. I failed Business because I lost all interest. I didn't let blogging take me over, but when I was feeling down, it gave me purpose where college made me feel like I had none. Still, I went to another college two years later and met amazing people there who also motivated me to continue with this blog.

I appreciate the support and encouragement I've received for this blog from my friends and family since I started on the 12th of October 2014. Unfortunately, with the blog put on hold, my writing temporarily paused during my studies, but the idea lives on, and the passion will never die.

However, almost ten years later, I'm still going down the dunes and going to places I never thought I'd be able to visit.

Even if you're thinking reading this: "Why should I listen to this guy?" I'll admit that is a fair question. I have been doing recreational Sandboarding since the age of 8. I have received invitations to attend Sandboarding events around the globe. I trained in France on the largest dune in Europe twice, and I have been blogging about the subject in a climate where there aren't a lot of sandboarding bloggers out on the web from a country with little to no sandboarding.

If there's one thing I've learned from this blog is that I'm happy to put time and effort into writing material that educates and informs; my blog might not be immortal, and there have been brief times where I've wanted to stop so this is also a reason why I'm writing this book.

I want to claim in this book that everything is to the best of my knowledge. I am not a legal expert or indeed qualified in law, writing, journalism, or any profession for that matter, I am simply an independent blogger that likes to go Sandboarding, and all opinions are my own.

I hope that in this book, you'll be able to discover my attitude and beliefs on practices, what I would and wouldn't do, my thoughts on places, and how also I can help you get involved in Sandboarding culture.

The writings in this book are a mix of opinion and consensus, but if you ever consider hitting a dune for some sandboarding, this book should be able to help you find your feet and get involved with the sport.

"Holywell Bay Sandboarding, Aged 16" by Jack Soley. All Rights Reserved.

Essential Equipment

As some of you may or may not be aware, my home country is Great Britain; I will admit that I have never witnessed such a Sandboarding following in this country, but it's something that sandboarders could exploit.

I mentioned that my original place to sandboard was Holywell Bay, but there are more places to go for a ride than Holywell. It's a valuable reminder that many places in the UK for dunes are on the coast; we are predominantly a cold country and just a lonely island.

Great Britain is known for being an island of tea drinkers, stunning scenery, haggis, fish and chips, and the Loch Ness monster, to name a few things. Alongside the spectacular views, the rivers, and the mountains, we have a few dunes in coastal places, so this is an extreme sport that can potentially have a following.

So how do you sandboard? It's a lot like snowboarding in the sense that you're not riding on compacted snow but loose sand; you may think that you might need to invest in expensive equipment and safety gear, but don't worry; you only need the essentials. There are optional pieces of equipment that may be of some use, but these are purely optional and unless you intend to compete in sporting events or sandboarding championships at some point in your life. Some of the articles in this list are more important than others; take note because these could potentially make the difference between you going home winning a trophy or even going home in an ambulance, for example.

Starter Boards

Having a sandboard is the most basic starting point for this sport. When starting on the dunes for the first time, you will probably discover that the cheap plastic boards you'll find in gift shops are the best boards to begin your sandboarding adventure. You can choose to opt for the round boards, these have the sole purpose for seated sandboarding, or you can try a traditionally shaped board that will let you stand. Still, you won't reach the speeds of a specialist sandboard, these are cheap, and I first discovered these when I started sandboarding and sadly, these were the only boards I used for over ten years before I purchased my first actual, purpose-built specialist board.

A specialist sandboard is a lot better in every way; you have no limits in the colours, shapes, designs, and foot straps you can have on the board. Unfortunately, there aren't too many sandboard makers out there, but if you manage to find one, you'll find they will sell you a sandboard, foot bindings, decals, as well as safety equipment and accessories as well.

"Sandboards" by ground.zero is licensed under CC BY 2.0

Buying New or Secondhand

You can either buy a secondhand sandboard as I did for the first time in 2019, but they are infrequent to come across, or you can buy one new. Buying a new board from abroad seems like a wise choice, but depending on where you are in the world, it could cost you a bomb in postage and import charges (I'll get onto such charges a little later in this book). The most popular sandboard makers are in sandboarding hot spots like North & South America, Australia, and South Africa because sandboarding is more common in those places. There is preexisting demand; whether it's for tour companies operating nearby or for sports schools, it shouldn't be of any surprise that the sandboard I purchased online was manufactured and imported from South Africa.

Prices for pre-owned boards start anywhere between £60 - £150. To some, it makes more financial sense to pay a little extra to buy a new board that may even give you some free goodies like some wax bars, and most definitely the peace of mind knowing your board's going to last for a long time before you end up buying your upgrade. In addition, some sandboarding merchants in other countries may offer a warranty on boards, something that you most definitely won't get when buying pre-owned.

"Sandboard Buried in Dune du Pilat" by Jack Soley is licensed under Creative CC BY-SA 4.0

I purchased my first sandboard from an online auction website for £60, described as "rarely used", and looking at the photos, the board looked neglected in a room for an extended period. So as soon as I saw a sandboard on sale, I asked the seller, "Do you have any more photos?" so I could inspect for any apparent damage and to make sure I wasn't the victim of a scam; the seller replied, almost immediately. So I bought it immediately, with no hesitation.

When you're looking at a secondhand sandboard, always look for scratches to inspect the condition; look at the bindings so that your feet can get on the board; and if they are adjustable, that's even better. Try looking at the size of the board as well; smaller sandboards are better for performing tricks and stunts, whereas longer ones tend to reach a faster speed.

Of course, with new sandboards, you don't need to inspect the boards personally, but I would recommend that you take these three steps:

1: Research the company. Does the company have good reviews from customers? Do customers buy more than once? Is the company long-standing? Does the company feel genuine?

2: If you're at a traditional brick and mortar store, ask the seller if you can try the board on a test ride, check if the bindings are comfortable, is the base of the board smooth? Is it big enough? Does it feel like it's sturdy? Again, the benefit of seeing the board in the flesh is that you know what you're paying for, and you don't need to pay shipping charges.

3: Can you return it in the unlikely event things don't work out? Is there a policy on returns for dissatisfaction? Obtaining a refund on a board may prove difficult if you buy online, as in some cases, the customer is liable for return shipping fees which is why some customers don't bother. Most jurisdictions will give consumers a grace period, but it's best to check with your local laws for guidance.

Importing Sandboards from Abroad

Morning broke on what I thought would be a good day; I got woke up by a loud knocking on my door, and I finally got my first ever brand new sandboard, fresh from the United States of America!

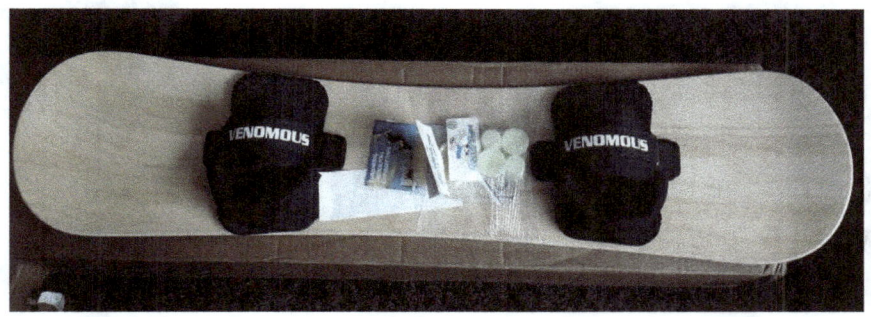

"Sport 120cm Sandboard Package" by Jack Soley is a public domain work.

Sandboard with Lustrum Bindings: $198.95 (£159.14)
Shipping to the UK: $89.80 (£71.83)
Total Cost: $288.75 (£230.97)

Exchange rate at time of purchase: £1 = $1.2502

I just went online and bought a standard sandboard from an online store; it just so happened to be Venomous Sandboards at Sand Master Park. Sand Master Park is a place that I have applauded so many times on my blog, and I was happy to buy from them because I'm familiar with their brand, and I know the quality they strive to achieve.

The benefits of buying from abroad are plentiful! The low prices for delivery and the board itself are one of them.

However, you might get a bit lucky buying a sandboard if you take advantage of exchange rates; for example, let's say you want to buy the Sandboard and Shipping for $300, if the rate is 1.28 dollars to the Pound Sterling, you'll be paying £234.38. Still, if you wait a week and the rate changes to 1.25 Dollars to the Pound Sterling, you'll now be paying £240. A difference of £5.62 might not be too appealing, but that difference could buy waxes or something else of good use! But on the flip side, if the exchange rates work against you, a difference this small might not be worth your time.

Also; Sandboarding is a niche sport, hence why the companies that make sandboards don't have a vast number of orders and why there are few merchants out there. Therefore, buying brand new products from sandboard sellers will not only support their livelihoods, but it'll keep the trade alive for people who want to purchase new sandboards (people who wish to upgrade or those who are new to the sport). Moreover, those profits can be re-invested to expand their services (i.e. Shipping to more countries or making bigger and better boards).

Before you get your credit card and buy yourself a big sandboard with the most comfortable bindings in the heat of the moment, don't let your guard down just yet; because someone who'll be waiting for your board to arrive just as much as you will be someone from your country's tax authority.

If we take my board as an example, the breakdown for the import charges was that I didn't pay any customs or excise duties (however, tax rules change all the time, and it depends on your country and the country you're importing from, so do your research!) But I had to pay £36.74 of Import VAT plus another £12 fee for clearance which is applied to "*help cover the cost of additional handling, administration, collection of monies and provision of facilities for Customs clearance of packages.*" (Parcelforce Worldwide, n.d.)

The cost of the delivery plus all import fees came to £120.57, which is 75.8% on top of the board's price; if you were to buy in the domestic market, the import charges wouldn't apply, and the shipping costs would be cheaper and in some cases, free of charge. Some countries, however, will let you take the board without any additional charge, and some countries will insist you pay a tax, plus another tax, and a fee on top of the taxes before you can even receive it. All countries have different tax policies, and because sandboards are pretty niche, countries will disagree on how they should be taxed.

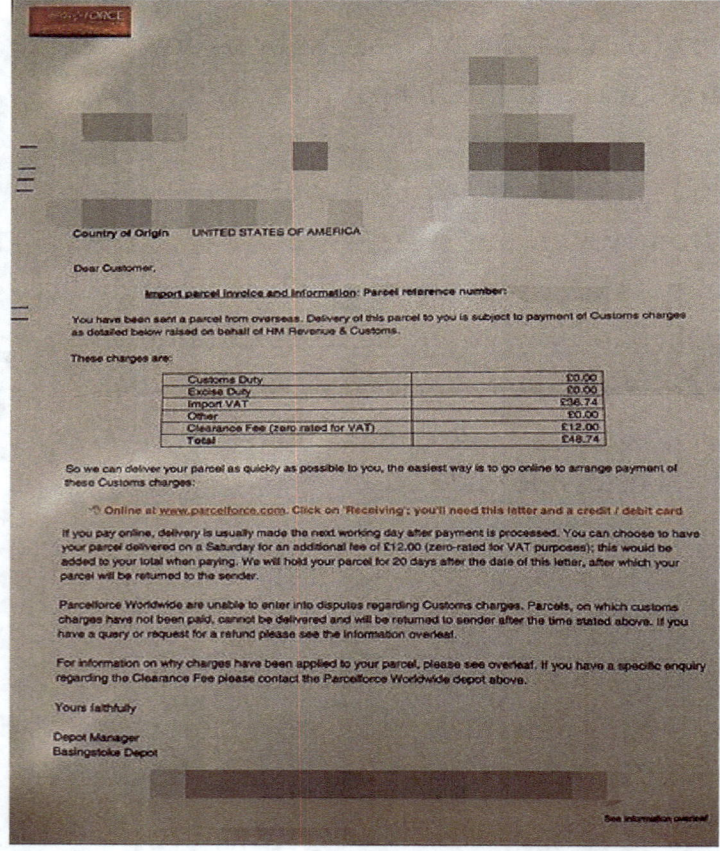

"Parcelforce Import Charge Invoice" by Jack Soley is a public domain work.

Quality can seriously determine whether or not you buy from one country or not; according to a survey of 43,034 respondents, goods made in Germany are the most reliable and goods made in China are the least reliable (Dalia Research, 2017). Still, suppose you're from a country with good standards of build quality, such as Canada, ranked 6th on this survey. In that case, it won't make sense to buy a sandboard from countries lower than you on the list, such as the United States and Australia (ranked 10th and 14th respectively), despite having a much bigger Sandboarding market.

If you're in a country with high manufacturing standards and reasonable quality control on goods, you know you're going to get a good quality product buying in the domestic market.

To conclude: Importing sandboards from other countries can support Sandboarding businesses around the world to provide more products and services to us, the public; whereas you'll have to pay around 75% more just for delivery and possible import charges, your country's sandboarding industry will ever so slightly decline while another country's sandboarding industry will ever so slightly improve; buying a Sandboard from abroad will give you more choice but you risk potentially worse build quality that might not last as long or perform as well as you would expect.

My experience with importing has been excellent; it was easy, and I'd happily do it again. However, the UK isn't a notable sandboarding country on the same scale as Australia, the USA, Egypt, or the UAE; therefore, there isn't a demand for British made sandboards. However, I don't have much choice as a British sandboarder. Given the positive reputation of British goods, I would give buying a domestically made sandboard a chance. If anyone reading this in the UK knows how to make a professionally made sandboard, get in touch; I'd like to be your next customer.

Using a Snowboard on Sand

A snowboard is a lot more common and widely available to purchase than a sandboard, partially because sandboarding is more niche and has fewer followers but primarily because there are dedicated snowboarding and ski resorts that people flock to in great numbers. If you're thinking of taking a snowboard to the dunes, be careful: a snowboard is designed to go down compact snow and is not for riding on an abrasive surface like sand; you could use a snowboard on a dune. However, there are some problems:

The first problem is that you won't reach the speed a normal sandboard would achieve; because the board is for riding on snow, not sand; so, if you're in a race down a dune with someone else on a sandboard; good luck.

The second problem is that they tend to get damaged more quickly because sand's abrasive properties eat away on the base of a snowboard a lot quicker. After all, it's not what a snowboard is for; also, using a snowboard on sand will most likely invalidate any warranty.

The final problem is also to do with the abrasiveness. For example, if you use a snowboard on sand; you'll find that as it eats the base of the board, therefore you will find it challenging to use it on a snow-capped mountain again and the speeds your board could once achieve on snow are now severely impaired because you decided to use it on the sand.

Snow wax is a product used on snowboards to help achieve faster speeds and better traction. There is wax for sandboards available on the market, but it's also worth noting that there are many alternatives to purchasing sandboard wax; my advice is that it's always best to look around for the best product. Alternatives for sandboarding wax I've seen people use are Beeswax, petroleum jelly, wax melts, and even crayons! (I will get onto waxes later in the book too!)

Ultimately, there are many variables: it all depends on whether the product you want is easily accessible; and the conditions of the dune you'll be riding on; how coarse or fine the sand will be, weather on the day, your weight, and wind direction, to name a few things that could affect your speed and agility.

There is some good news in all of this; other equipment you'll find for snowboards will be just fine for sandboarding, whether it's goggles, helmets, bindings, knee pads, etc. Just ensure that sandboards stay on the sand and snowboards stay on snow.

Goggles

I don't know about you, but I would rather keep my eyes in good condition; the best and obvious way to do this is to wear goggles or specific glasses in your sport of choice. For wearing goggles for Sandboarding, I think you run into a bit of an awkward situation here because you need to find goggles that will prevent sand from entering your eye area. Unfortunately, it isn't easy to find perfect goggles. Some sand can be as small as 10 micrometres and invisible to the naked eye; for comparison, the largest bacterium ever discovered is the "*Thiomargarita namibiensis*" is still more prominent in size than a grain of medium sand. However, that specific bacterium is visible to the naked eye.

Considering this, if a manufacturer of specialist goggles claims to prevent all sand from entering your eyes, I would think it would be a scam as it sounds too good to be true. But, of course, it could be theoretically possible that someone could invent a pair of goggles with the ability to block particles in the future. For example, if you were to fall off your board and hit the dune head first, your head would hit the dune with such impact that the elastic on the back of the goggles would compress and expand. A wipeout on the dune would let sand in from your hair find its way into your eyelids, even if the goggles managed to stay on your head.

The pair of goggles I purchased in a charity shop a few years ago has a spongy area around my eyes to protect them against incoming sand particles. My goggles also have a rubberised strap on the back, so the goggles don't slip off my abnormal head, and they have a UV protective lens. It's a good solution for now, but I would be sure to invest in an upgrade in the future.

"Sport goggles" by Peter Dutton is licensed under CC BY 2.0

In many places where sandboarding takes place, it's on a nice day, and the sun is out, so another hazard that's of consideration when you're out on the dunes is that of ultraviolet rays.

According to the Met Office in the UK, the leading cause of blindness is the development of cataracts. Long-term exposure to UV rays is severe, and exposure to UV rays is a risk factor for cataract development. Ultraviolet can also burn the eye's surface tissue a lot, like sunburn on the skin, including other eye parts such as the cornea and lens.

To summarise, I would go for a pair of goggles that are good at keeping foreign objects and debris out and deflecting harmful UV rays.

Helmets

In 2019, I wrote an article on the best helmets to use in Sandboarding; it started like this: "*In November 2016, the wearing of helmets was made mandatory in all InterSands Sandboarding events with a unanimous vote from members and athletes from Chile, Argentina, Brazil, Peru, and Switzerland.*" (Soley, J. 2019)

A lot like riding a motorcycle in many jurisdictions, helmet usage in Sandboarding is mandatory when you're competing in some events. However, wearing helmets is not required when you're recreationally sandboarding in a public area.

In snowboarding, wearing a helmet makes logical sense as the snow is compact, solid, and often frozen. In addition, snow-capped mountains are not the best place to fall on; however, in Sandboarding, wearing a helmet still makes sense. The consequences of falling over on a dune are not as severe because the sand is very light, it's loose, and you potentially only have the opportunity to hurt your head if you fall on your board or discover a piece of debris on a dune. If your helmet is light, you should be okay as long as a protective shell exists over your head.

"Casques" by RSCT is licensed under CC BY-SA 3.0

It's good to wear a helmet. Unfortunately, in the recorded sandboarding deaths I had measured in my blog post "Revisiting Death", some of the deaths were accidents; regardless of whether the participants had been wearing helmets, it's unknown whether or not they would have survived. As I write this book, there has not been a single death in sandboarding that is directly related to the absence of wearing protective headgear but don't let that convince you that you won't be next; it's good to have some form of protection and could just as well save your life.

There isn't a specific helmet for sandboarding, but a snowboarding helmet will suffice, as will a skateboarding helmet. I would recommend wearing a helmet with reinforced padding or sturdy material to resist impacts; try going for helmets with complex compounds such as ABS, EPS foam or lightweight polycarbonate. Finally, for added safety points, try looking for a helmet that meets a certain safety standard; ideally, a European, BSI or ASTM certification; many helmets sold in certain countries for most sports will need these requirements by law anyway.

Another good feature to find on a helmet is air vents, they work best when you're at speed, and comfort pads inside the helmet can absorb sweat.

Pads

I would also say something about additional pads such as knee pads, shin pads, or elbow pads; however, I don't use them, and I feel like knee and elbow pads hinder my performance from doing tricks (which I will cover later in this book). But, protectors on the knees and elbows can help when you're sandboarding, especially if you intend to go well over 50kph (~30mph).

"Nicolas Mahut volley RG 2012" by Carine06 is licensed under CC BY-SA 2.0

Bags

You might be thinking to yourself: "Bags don't sound like an essential item for sandboarding." And you'd be correct, but before you skip over this part, I want to present you a question: Imagine you're going to take a flight from New York to Los Angeles to do some sandboarding in the Mojave Desert, how do you make sure your sandboard in the aircraft's hold luggage stays safe and doesn't get lost? Would you risk leaving your board exposed?

The advantages of having a bag for your sandboard go further beyond ease of transportation. Many bags made for sandboards will have a shoulder strap, which is convenient and easy to carry around; some bags even have small zip pockets to include accessories like goggles, cameras, etc. Even if you have some more room in the primary bag, you will most of the time be able to fit a helmet and maybe some more clothes inside.

In my opinion, sandboard and snowboard bags are again very similar if not the same; they fit a sandboard plus some extras, they're easy to carry, so in my opinion, they must be the same. Not only is a bag for a board better for transportation, but it keeps it tidier and makes you look more organised.

"Sandboard Equipment at Night" by Jack Soley is licensed under CC BY-SA 4.0

Waxes

I mentioned snowboard waxes earlier in this book, and yes, there are waxes on the market that will gain you more speed when you're surfing down a dune as well!

Professionally made waxes will set you back more money as they are for Sandboarding; however, alternatives are cheaper and may even do a better job than professionally made products.

I have experimented with some waxes, and the best in my experience to date is Beeswax, a natural wax produced by bees used as a protector of wooden products. Suitable wax products used by the professionals will have been rigorously tested for Sandboarding and may not damage the board over time as some substitutes. Unfortunately, there hasn't been any long term research into waxes for Sandboarding and what can happen to your board over prolonged use.

Aside from Beeswax, other waxes that can help you go down dunes faster include Wax melts, crayons, surfers' wax, and car wax.

"Pure Natural Beeswax Blocks" by Jack Soley is licensed under CC BY-SA 4.0

Cameras

Once again, this is not a core essential to sandboarding, but imagine you want to flex on your friends and show them how cool of a sandboarding enthusiast you are; how would you go about showing everyone how good you are at surfing down a dune? You'd film it, of course!

A camera I use is a knock-off of a very well-known action camera brand that I purchased in 2015. For a product made in China and sold as an imitation of a particular camera (we all know what brand of camera it is, and I knew it was an imitation when I bought it), it's still working as I write this book. Unfortunately, the accessory pack I bought with the camera has broken parts already, so the camera has outlived the accessories.

"GoPro camera mounted on car" by Maksym Kozlenko is licensed under CC BY-SA 4.0

The accessories you can get for these action cameras are mounts for various body parts, sticky pads to attach to helmets/equipment, handlebar mounts for bikes, suction mounts, spare batteries, and waterproof housing, to name a few. So if you can think of something valuable that you might need for a camera, the chances are that you'll be able to find it for sale.

Those are, in my belief, the essential requirements to sandboard in pretty much any environment, and I will go over the prices of my goods and where I got them from, this could be beneficial if you look in charity shops, jumble sales, etc. You can find bargains as you've never seen before, but the choice is ultimately yours. When you're looking at the prices, consider that the dates when I bought them are different, the costs may fluctuate, and some of the products that I've described may not be available anymore. I won't include the brand names because if I do, I could get lawyers at my front door, and that's an inconvenience I'd rather not have.

- Sandboard: Advanced composite & Epoxy fibreglass board, purchased preowned online in February 2019 for £60 (or a new Sandboard for £230.97 in January 2020)
- Goggles: Ski/Snowboard goggles with anti-fog treatment and anti-scratch lens coating, purchased

preowned from a charity shop in Gloucester, England in June 2017 for £1.99

- Helmet: BMX/Skate Helmet, with lightweight ABS shell and air vents, purchased new online in March 2019 for £9.99

- Pads: Knee & Elbow Pads, purchased new online whilst I was on holiday in India (yes, really) in October 2017 for 499 Rupees

- Bag: Waterproof "Snowboard" Luggage Bag Case, measuring 155cm, purchased new online in March 2019 for £21.97

- Waxes: Beeswax, locally sourced, purchased online with free shipping; 6 bars for £2.99

- Camera: 1080p 30fps Action Camera with Wi-Fi connectivity, included with accessory kit, purchased new online in August 2015 for £71 (£45 for the camera, £18 for the accessory kit, and £8 for total delivery charges)

How to be a Sandboarder

There isn't a defined term for a sandboarder or a person who rides down dunes. Still, when I started my blog back in 2014, I called it "Sandboarding Nation" because I had the belief that people who are into sandboarding are known as a community or a group with a common bond, a bit like a tribe and what's another word for a tribe? Nation.

Unlike other sports, sandboarding doesn't have an exam or test to reach a certain level to be certified as a bona fide sportsperson in a specific sport. You can go down a dune fast or slow, do tricks if you want, race, and even try some small jumps. The aim of sandboarding, in my opinion, is to be considerate towards each other, be aware of the environment around us as rare wildlife and plants are notable near dunes, and to enjoy our time sandboarding on the dunes.

However, this doesn't necessarily mean that sandboarding is purely recreational; there are competitions in varying disciplines (stunts and racing), a lot like snowboarding. A variety of disciplines and events is why a lot of snowboarders would be very familiar with sandboarding, and even 4-time Sandboarding world champion Josh Tenge "*got into sandboarding in '97 and was introduced to it through a couple snowboard buddies.*" (Romantic Oregon Coast Vacations, n.d.)

It's no surprise that people who are previously associated with snowboarding tend to be good sandboarders as well. An excellent example of a snowboarder making waves in sandboarding is Alex Bird, a sandboarding teacher featured in a 2017 television commercial to break the UK land speed record on a sandboard. Alex, who has skied since the age of 3, also got into skateboarding and then snowboarding at around age 11; Alex has become hooked onto all kinds of board sports; Sandboarding included. (Soley, J. 2019)

There are many qualities to being a sandboarder, and not one sandboarding athlete is the same as another; not all will become world champions. However, all sandboarders will have a backstory on how they got into the sport; unlike Alex Bird & Josh Tenge, I did not have a background in other sports. I just returned to the dunes every summer sandboarding; it was the only sport I felt comfortable doing. Many years have gone by, and now I have gained a driving licence; I can continue my passion instead of just waiting for every summer to pass by. In this chapter, I want to give some general advice on being a good sportsperson and developing and increasing skills over time.

Performing Tricks

It's all well and good going down a dune in a straight line; I can tell you I even get a buzz from doing just that. Over time, and especially if you want to enter the competitive world, it's worth you trying to get into the realm of performing stunts on your board. As with anything, it's best to start small.

I can tell you hand on heart; I can't do a wheelie when I ride a bike. My cautious side takes over, and I instinctively fight hard to get back onto the ground. But when it comes to grabbing my board and doing a front flip up a ramp, I'm all for it!

I started by doing little jumps off dune tops to see if I could safely land, then I moved on to jumping as I was coming down the dune; I bought a small ramp for this. Then I moved onto, seeing if I could grab the board. Before I made a successful flip, it took wipe-outs, crashes, and many hours of practice.

I give you, in my opinion, the most valuable chart I've ever come across in my whole time since I started Sandboarding, and probably one of the most helpful things in this book. The diagram below shows all the possible tricks you can do on a sandboard. Then, following the most beneficial visual in the world is a photo of yours truly, riding "Mute" back in 2019.

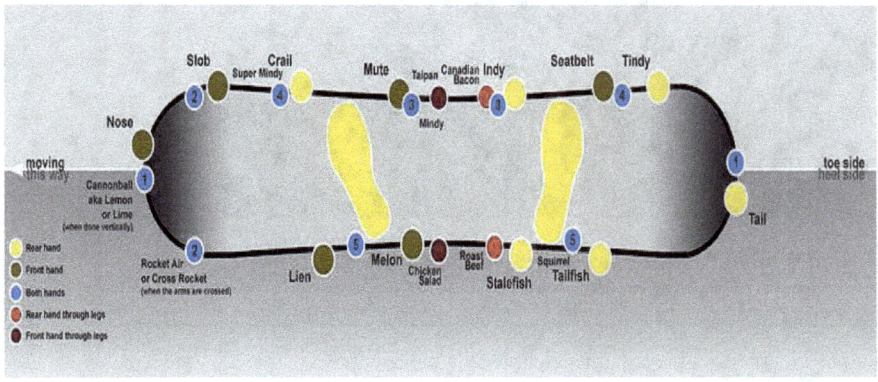

"Snowboard illustrated grabs" by Nlin86 is licensed under CC BY-SA 3.0.

"Sandboarding Mute" by Jack Soley is licensed under CC BY-SA 3.0.

Speed and Direction Control

If the wind speed isn't offensive and there aren't obstacles in your way, this is your golden opportunity to learn how to control your speed and direction on the dune.

The general rule is to lean toward the board's nose to go faster and lean toward the tail if you want to slow down;

raising your arms can also assist this by increasing drag and air resistance.

When it comes to controlling your sandboard direction, I ride a natural stance (left foot first), lean forwards to turn right, and shift my weight back to turn left; this is the other way round if you ride a goofy stance (right foot first). Lean too little, and you won't change your direction; lean too much, you'll lose your balance and fall in the sand.

Preparing yourself physically

I cannot talk much about this, my stamina has been quite bad for a lot of my younger life, and I have rarely known myself to be a physical person. I'm not overweight, but I'm not the best person in a tank top either; my stamina and endurance have always been a problem for me, and I'm not ashamed to admit that.

A notable reason why sandboarding is less popular than its icy counterpart is that there are no chair lifts to take you to the top of a dune; "*it is very difficult to build a mechanised ski lift on a sand dune, and so participants must walk back up to the top. Alternatively, they may ride a dune buggy or all-terrain vehicle back to the top of the dune.*" (Eleftheriou, D. 2012)

Some people may think that this is a good reason why sandboarding is better, it's more involving because you're not reliant on a chair lift taking you to the top of a dune, and you have to do some work to get to the top, but once you go down the dune, I think the hard effort is worth it.

Ever since I started doing sandboarding more often, I realised that there is no such thing as a Sandboarding athlete. You don't need to be in peak physical condition to become a professional sandboarder, but it helps when you're walking up a steep dune on a hot day. Before I proceed with my recommendations, I am not a health professional, and the following is what I do, everyone is different, so there are different needs for other people.

Building Leg Muscles

The main reason why so many people lag or feel sluggish in sandboarding is the sheer amount of work you have to do in order to just 'survive' (realistically enjoy it). I would think that building your leg muscles to make climbing the dune easier would be a good start; I would imagine that doing at least 45 minutes of walking, running or an hour cycling in a day would usually make more noticeable leg muscles in a short while. This would be a great place to start on your personal development especially if you're in a place without the use of an off-road vehicle.

Stamina

I have always had a problem with my stamina and endurance until about 2019; a suitable method I've done to boost my stamina is Interval training. For example, I will do a brisk walk or light jog for 2 minutes, but I will run faster for 90 seconds. I have discovered that 'cardiovascular' workouts attempt to make your heart function in oxygen-deprived (anaerobic) conditions. I have done the research, and your maximum aerobic (with oxygen) heart rate, at which you can perform and operate well to burn fat and increase your levels of stamina, and endurance, work out to be your 180 minus your age. I wouldn't exceed your maximum heart rate; I'd go no more than 10% below it for an efficient workout. Stamina is something to work on in this sport as you have to climb up the dune to surf down it in most cases.

Diet

Just eat the right foods and drink good drinks. I would find it essential to have a good breakfast of cereal or a modest-sized cooked breakfast at least two and a half hours before your sandboarding session to give your body time to process the food down and for a chance to 'relieve yourself' as it were. If you don't have the time for a sensible breakfast, I find a nice bowl of porridge works well. I would, under all circumstances, avoid high stimulant energy drinks, carbonated drinks, sugary drinks, and energy drinks as they cause you to crash and burn later in the day and could mean trouble to you being awake. In contrast, coffee and tea-related beverages slowly release energy and are better.

Water Consumption

I cannot stress enough how vital it is to get water and a lot of it! Of course, water consumption is different for many people, and some factors involve gender, weight, height, diet, how often you sweat, etc., but for every hour I'm on the dunes on a hot summer's day in England, I use roughly 500ml.

Sleep

It's always beneficial to get a good night's sleep; there are multiple opinions and debates on how many hours of sleep you should be getting; my research tells me that the most widely accepted answer is 7.5 or 8 hours per night. There are smartphone apps that will effectively measure your average sleep cycles and inform you when the best time is to wake up or go to sleep to wake up feeling fresh and energised. One 'sleep cycle' typically lasts 90 minutes, and 5 or 6 cycles per night are accepted to be a 'good night's sleep'; waking up in the middle of a sleep cycle and not after one has finished is the number one reason why people tend to be sluggish when they wake up from sleep. So five sleep cycles are good because there are usually 90 minutes in a sleep cycle, and 90 times five is 450, convert 450 minutes into hours gives you an answer of 7.5 hours. On the other hand, a lack of sleep can increase the risk of heart attacks and suicide; plus, if you're taking part in recreational or competitive sandboarding, it can cause you to lose focus.

"Sleeping man in Ouagadougou" by Roman Bonnefoy is licensed under CC BY-SA 3.0

Aerodynamics (Shaving Legs)

This section isn't essential for this part of the book, but I've included it because it sounds interesting. There is a common misconception that cyclists in the annual 'Tour de France' shave their legs because of aerodynamics. The fact that shaving your legs will make you go faster is correct, but in a stage of the Tour De France, for example, it doesn't make a lot of difference. My thinking and logic behind this 'shaving legs theory' is that it could work on the dunes, but only by a few nanoseconds I haven't done any personal research into this, and I don't think anyone else has either. Swimmers with shaved legs also have reported a slight advantage in the water as drag is ever so slightly decreased.

Aside from aerodynamics, If you need to clean yourself or need to apply a plaster, it's much easier on a leg with no hair, and I've also received a tip-off that women love men with smooth legs.

Mindset

I've talked about what to do physically and mentally. Still, I forgot one key element, whether you're Sandboarding for recreation or in a competition, you need to have the right mentality. You want to be a part of the sport; you want to get involved; if you lack interest, you won't appreciate the experience as much. But, on the other hand, if you say to yourself that you want to have an excellent time on the dunes or win a sandboarding contest, you'll motivate yourself to go a little further!

Persistence

This topic is my final piece on this chapter, and probably the one that shows your level of commitment to the sport is your persistence. If your stamina is awful like mine, you don't have a sense of balance, or you live a long-distance away. However, you still come back to dunes for some recreational sandboarding, which is a quality that shows your commitment to sandboarding and shows your strength as a person. I remember back when I was

20 years old; on my days off when I wasn't working night shifts in a petrol station or studying during the day at college, I got in my car and drove for 2 hours to South Wales and 2 hours back home.

Even when I don't own a car, I every once in a while borrow my mum's car, and I'll drive to Wales in the morning, and I'll be home for the evening. However, if you put in a level of commitment as some sportspeople put in their sport of choice, you'll be recognised for your talents even if you're not necessarily 'good'. For example, take Eric "The Eel" Moussambani of Equatorial Guinea, who I see as a personal hero. Moussambani was a man who had never seen an Olympic sized swimming pool and had only taken up swimming eight months before the Sydney Olympic Games in 2000. Moussambani swam the 100m freestyle and won his heat in the slowest time in Olympic history. Yet, he set a national record for Equatorial Guinea and later became the national swimming coach of his country.

There is no one-size-fits-all sandboarder, we're all different, and there are other circumstances for different people, and who knows, you might even turn out to be the best sandboarder alive.

Sandboarding Knowledge and Understanding

If you're going to try your hand at this sport, it makes perfect sense to try and know some of the history and origins of the sport as well; I can't remember how many times I've had to explain Sandboarding to other people. Some people go further and ask questions such as "Who invented it?" and "How did it become popular?" both of which are excellent questions and ones I have investigated for the answers. This part of the book aims to dig deeper at the big questions relating to the sport, so if you get asked by anyone, you can come up with an informed and intelligent answer.

What is Sandboarding?

As the name would imply, sandboarding is snowboarding, but instead, on a snow-capped mountain, it's on a dune. This exact wording is what I use whenever anyone looks at me confused whenever I say I do sandboarding. So sandboarding is what it says in the name, snowboarding but on the sand.

When was Sandboarding invented?

There's a distinction between ancient and modern Sandboarding; I'll look at ancient Sandboarding first: there are many answers to this. There's no universally accepted correct answer, but I'll look at two potential contenders. The first possibility goes to Ancient Egypt, where it has alleged on hieroglyphics that "*people would use wooden planks or pieces of pottery for faster travel and for transporting cargo across the sand dunes.*" (Old Town Inn. 2019)

It's worth mentioning that there have been no sources of

these events or depictions of Sandboarding on hieroglyphics as of yet. Furthermore, because Egypt is one of the cradles of civilization, it's unknown who was the first pharaoh or peasant to take some wood or clay and go down a dune. Therefore, we can't give one individual the title 'Inventor of Sandboarding'.

It then leads us to China in the Middle Ages, where there was a "*Chinese ritual where sliding down the dunes in a similar fashion around 800 AD*' (Sandboard Magazine, n.d.) Again, there is not enough concrete evidence to support this theory.

Now onto the modern sport, that can go to one of 2 places, the first goes to Brazil. "*Modern, upright sandboarding is believed to have been invented in Brazil in the 1940s. In recent years, though, advances in materials and techniques have led to much faster speeds and longer jumps than ever imagined before; professional sandboarders routinely reach speeds in excess of 60 mph (100 kph) and jump distances of 50 feet (15m) or more.*" (Kissell, J. 2019.)

The story, if confirmed, would mean that surfers of Brazil,

specifically Santa Catarina, would go sandboarding "*as an alternative to surfing if there were low, or no tidal waves.*" (Actionhub Reporters, 2017)

The second possible contender is the United States; "*there are stories of people in the 50's riding car hoods down the dunes in California and people on sand boards getting pulled behind cars on the beach in Oregon, USA.*" (Sengers, M. 2017)

But there's also Dr Dune in Oregon, who on his website states that: "*I myself started sandboarding on a slalom water ski in 1972 and was introduced to this sport by friends who were sliding down the dunes on similar planks in the early 60's. I have seen photos of people standing up on boards with no bindings from the 50's but, again, these were devises all ready in existence for other sports or other purposes and simply tried out on the sand.*" (Sandboard Magazine, n.d.)

It's worth mentioning that these 'boards' aren't for surfing on sand; they were often snowboards, waterboards, or boards suited to other sports; the account from Dr Dune also strengthens another claim: "*What is known is that sand boarding has been developing as a thriving sport since the early 60's. People were sliding down dunes on planks and standing up on boards with no bindings."* (Sengers, M. 2017).

As there is no universally accepted answer, my opinion is that in ancient times, Sandboarding was most likely, an Egyptian invention. Still, in the modern age, Sandboarding was revived and re-invented in either the United States or Brazil between 1940 and 1970. There's still a bit of debate if modern Sandboarding is an American or Brazilian sport, and both countries try to out-do one another as to who invented it.

The Etymology of Sandboarding

The word itself is relatively new for some reason because the popularity of the sport only took off quite recently. The Oxford English Dictionary first noted 'sandboarding' as a noun, and 'sandboard' as both a noun & a verb as late as 2004, and 'snowboarding' was first recorded as late as 2002, despite it being introduced at the Winter Olympics in Nagano 4 years before its inclusion in the Oxford English Dictionary. Both of the new entries are one-worded (without hyphens).

According to Google's Ngram viewer, where the frequency of words; have been recorded in past works, "sandboarding" & "sand boarding" was first referenced in 1924. The first reference did not mean the sport that is the subject of this book. In 1963, 'sandboarding' was first used with the meaning that relates to our sport and pastime. The official definition of sandboarding is: "*a recreational activity resembling snowboarding but performed on sand instead of snow.*" (YourDictionary, n.d.)

Is there a competitive element to Sandboarding?

In short, yes, in the same way, you have Snowboarding competitions. The first Sandboarding competition was the Sand Master Jam at Sand Master Park in 1996; it's an annual event that continues today.

Other well-known examples include the Sandboarding World Championship that takes place annually in Hirschau, Germany & the Sandboard World Cup, hosted by the Intersands International Sandboarding and Sandski Association, which takes place every two years.

These competitions and events incorporate many elements of a Snowboarding event such as freestyle, rails, races, and slaloms.

Globalisation of the Sport

Two organisations govern the sport, one of them is the 'Intersands International Sandboarding and Sandski Association' and the other is 'Dune Riders International'.

According to its Facebook Page, Dune Riders International is "*the governing body for international amateur and professional competitive sandboarding.*" (Dune Riders International, 2021) The headquarters for D.R.I. is at Sand Master Park in Oregon, which is also convenient as the Sand Master Park itself; hosts 2 of the events on the Dune Riders International World Tour.

The mission is to provide structure and support for the competitive and recreational aspects of Sandboarding, also according to the Director of Dune Riders International: "*DRI's fundamental purpose, as set forth in its by-laws, is to seek and implement effective means to utilize and preserve the dune systems of the world as well as educate the public regarding the sport of sandboarding as a healthy, safe and fun activity for all peoples in all lands.*" (Dune Riders International, 2021)

The other organisation is Intersands, based in Switzerland, and their mission is as follows: "*Through the development of sandboarding and sandski, we want to expand outdoor sports activities, starting to create a sports culture in the little ones. We think that by strengthening the development of these two disciplines with adequate equipment and the technical guidance of professionals as applied in snowboarding and skiing, we will create in future generations a sports culture open to any habitat, whether on the sand or in the snow.*" (Intersands, n.d.)

Both international organisations hold competitive events in their own right. However, there appears to be no standardisation in how the organisations have events. Still, realistically, there seems to be not much difference between how these two organisations operate.

Issues Facing Sandboarding Today

We already know Sandboarding is a niche sport. It's not very well known, and even well-known sports like football (or soccer for the Americans) have their problems such as hooliganism and VAR. I want to dig deeper into the potential difficulties presented to Sandboarding. I won't be able to fix them, but by merely addressing them, I hope that the problems in Sandboarding will find solutions one day in the future.

You Can't Buy Equipment

If you're looking to get involved in any sport, you know where to find equipment and appropriate clothes, but the problem with Sandboarding is that there's no particular location or shop where you can buy goods. There are some small outlets in places near dunes, but if you go to any sports shop in the city, it'll be unlikely that you'll find Snowboarding goods, so you can suspect that it'll be much more challenging to find Sandboarding goods.

First off, you need to use a Sandboard; this is because a snowboard has a layer that allows itself to glide effectively on snow and frozen surfaces. However, sand has abrasive qualities and therefore gets rid of the said layer, giving rise to an unwritten rule among Sandboarders that if you use a Snowboard on the sand, you can only use it on sand from then on. However, this claim has not yet had verification as no studies or tests have taken place with scientific backing.

There aren't many good places for Sandboarding

There aren't as many locations for sandboarding to take place; I'll admit that there are fixed locations for snowboarding, but when the weather turns cold and starts to snow, a lot of hills and mountains would be snowboard friendly. Still, unfortunately, sand doesn't come from the sky, so sandboarding must occur at a fixed location, mainly in the desert or on beaches.

For example, the total area of dunes in England & Wales is just shy of 200 square kilometres (Doody, P. 2019), roughly the size of American Samoa. For comparison, the Great Sand Dunes National Park in Colorado, USA, has an area 3 times larger (just over 600 square kilometres and roughly the same size as Saint Lucia) (U.S. Department of the Interior, n.d.)

The problem lies with the fact that many dune systems around the world are protected and ban recreational activities from taking place, either because of concerns regarding coastal erosion or rare wildlife in the area.

Some authorities ban sandboarding for other reasons. Reasons for prohibiting sandboarding include concerns with tourists who litter the place and ruin it for the rest of us, problems with safety, it's on an international border, or because the dunes by some people and cultured are regarded as sacred and must not be disturbed.

Demand for Sandboarding is Low

The market for Sandboarding is nowhere near what the market is for snowboarding despite the sport being virtually the same. Just the engineering logistics of establishing a sandboarding park would be challenging as a chair lift, for example, would be extremely difficult, if not impossible, due to the shifting sands. The same could apply to building pretty much anything on a dune, except for one place, the Sand Master Park in Oregon, USA.

This park is a haven for Sandboarding not only because it has a vast area of dunes that look out to the Pacific Ocean. Sand Master Park also hosts tuition for beginners, board hire, and their shop with pretty much every bit of merchandise you can think of for Sandboarding. However, even with a success story like Sand Master Park, I believe that the demand for Sandboarding is low because only one location in the United States is a specialist park. In addition, it's expensive to buy decent equipment. Unless you live near a coast or in the desert, the barriers to entry are high for the average adrenaline addict, so most tend not to bother investing in the equipment and hire a sandboard while they're on holiday.

Because there's not too much demand for Sandboarding, there isn't a need to establish marketing to promote the sport. For instance, you will find video games that feature Snowboarding, Jet skiing, and even Skateboarding as the primary sport. Still, I've yet to see a video game released that's purely dedicated to Sandboarding. I have seen games that have minor elements that feature Sandboarding as a mini-game or a challenge, such as *Tak & The Power of Juju*, a game that came to consoles in

2003, other games were never released that utilised Sandboarding as the primary aim.

There's not a lot of Events

If you're a keen footballer, you'll try to make a football team, and if you're a terrific footballer, you'll probably receive an invite to play for the national side.

But if you're an excellent sandboarder, you might get asked to take part in the one or two international sandboarding events that take place every year. If you're from somewhere relatively isolated from the sandboarding world, like the United Kingdom, for instance, you'll find that when you look for Sandboarding events near you, you'll get a big fat nothing. However, if I was looking for the same thing but in the United States, Australia and some other nations, I'll get a higher chance of success.

The nearest Sandboarding event near me would be the events organised by Dune Riders International at Curracloe, Ireland, as part of its Sandboard World Tour; there's also Sandspirit Festival annually at Monte Kaolino in Bavaria.

Unless I hosted an event myself (which would look highly unethical if I took part and won), I'd have to travel internationally to participate in a Sandboarding event.

It's hard to get Insurance

Buying Travel Insurance won't apply to you unless you're medically invincible. Still, suppose you're going out for a session on the dunes. In that case, it's always a good idea to get medical insurance. If you're travelling, make sure that you're covered for Sandboarding in your Travel Insurance as not many insurance companies will cover you due to the obscure nature of the sport.

In January 2020, I got 76 quotes for an annual travel insurance premium and only 41% of those covered me if I were to go Sandboarding and this tells me one of three things about the insurers:

- Insurance companies don't recognise Sandboarding as a sport, and the sheer majority of customers have most likely never been Sandboarding

- Sandboarding, with its undocumented low injury rate, isn't considered as a big enough risk for insurance companies to make a profit

- Insurance companies recognise Sandboarding as a sport, but insurers decide that it's not worth the risk because of its niche nature.

My conclusion of travel insurance is that it's good if you're unfortunate enough to be injured on a Sandboarding excursion; operations and medical procedures can be costly in some places, but the travel insurance is very cheap. (Soley, J. 2020)

Sandboarding Deaths

I was very close to not putting it in the book, but I had to address this. It's unfortunate when someone dies doing a sport someone loves best. However, anyone who tells you that Sandboarding, in particular, is very deadly is, to put it bluntly, a liar.

In the year 2019, 90 cyclists died on UK roads. (Department for Transport, 2019)

In that same year, there were 42 fatalities in ski & snowboarding resorts in the United States. (Persall, F. n.d.)

But the statistics for deaths and injuries for Sandboarding can be outdated at best and non-existent at worst. In an old blog post, I stated that Sandboarding had an average of 0.45 deaths per year as of 2019. I drew another conclusion that Sandboarding is safer than Table Tennis, with only seven recorded deaths from table tennis between 1997 and 2006, but that respective study took place in Germany. In contrast, the five publicised sandboarding deaths between 2009 and 2019 took place in New Zealand, Namibia, and Peru.

It's unlikely that this happens regularly. However, there are ways during a sport where death is approaching: whether it's a freak accident by colliding into someone or something, coming into contact with hazardous animals, plants, or materials, natural disasters, extreme heat, extreme cold, or even pre-existing medical conditions which could trigger a bigger problem. My top tips to prevent serious injuries include:

- Always be aware of your surroundings when you're on the dunes and keep an eye out for anything suspicious; plan whenever possible by looking out for weather forecasts and potential safe places.

- Don't go too fast. If you're a beginner on the dunes, try going halfway up to the summit so you won't be able to achieve a faster speed coming down, this works because you still get to reach a suitable speed where you feel exhilarated coming down, and you don't have to walk up as high.

- Know your limits. If you're exhausted, or you're not confident about slowing down after a certain speed, or you feel like you're losing control of your slide, take a break.

- Know about problems before you go Sandboarding. Whether it's medical problems that may be more challenging after sport, or especially if you're going to an exotic location, get immunised for illnesses prominent abroad; the most common ones are Hepatitis and Malaria.

Potential injury and death is understandably a morbid subject. Still, if we discuss it, we can do as much as possible to prevent it, and if you're still worried about Sandboarding killing you, remember that 150 people a year are killed by falling coconuts. (Fone, M. 2019)

Interviews With Sandboarders

If you're in a sport that involves teams, you're most likely going to have a good relationship with the players on your team, some players are even good friends with their traditional rivals, and they see the sport as a way to socialise, make friends, and have a good time. So my mission is to try and get to know as many Sandboarding professionals and people who are 'in the know' as I can.

Alex Bird

The first interview I ever did as part of my blog was with Alex Bird, an extreme sportsman who's also a Sandboarding instructor; this interview came about when he starred in a television commercial where an SUV towed him on the dunes.

- How did you initially get into sports?

"I have skied since I was 3 years old. I then got into skateboarding and then snowboarding from the age of about 11, since then I've been hooked on all board sports."

- Would this partially be the reason why you got into sandboarding as well?

"Yeah the excitement of going sideways! I enjoyed team sports too but love the freedom and adventure that go with board sports."

- In 2017, you were approached by Jeep for their Renegade Desert Hawk, how did it feel to be a part of that?

"It was a really exciting project and an honour to be involved in, Jeep approached us asking what sort of things could be done, we talked through lots of ideas including trying to break the sandboarding speed record, they were really supportive with our ideas."

- Has anyone recognised you from the advert?

"No! Although we do sandboarding lessons and people who book have often seen the ad."

- Have you done sandboarding in other places?

"I've been to Dune Du Pilat in France, which is awesome and has some of the longest runs I've had but I think we have a bit more variety and some different features to ride."

- Would sandboarding be a sport you want more people to know about?

"Definitely. It's a great activity and a great way to stay fit! It also happens in some beautiful places, events are always a great way to inspire and get more people involved in the sport."

- Are you competitive?

"I can be! I compete in the British Kitesurfing Championships Wavemasters Fleet, I've come 3rd for the last 2 years. It can really motivate and push you to improve."

- Any long term ambitions?

"Just to see my kids get better than me!"

- What advice would you give to anyone who wants to start in a competitive sport?

"Get involved and enjoy it. Be honest with yourself and others about your own ability and people will support you. I've met some great people and learnt loads through competition."

Vitor Semedo

Vitor Semedo is a regular competitor in the Sandboard World Cup; in 2017, he finished 3rd in the Boardercross discipline for Cabo Verde; and in 2019, he came 2nd in the Slalom and was crowned world champion in Boardercross. I was lucky enough to interview him after his win.

- How does it feel to be world champion in Boardercross?

"I still can't believe that I can call myself world champion, I did a bronze medal in 2017 and I was there more for the experience than for the title!"

- What do you think you did differently this time to be the world champion as opposed to coming 3rd?

"Work, training, practice, and fun were the added ingredients."

- How would you prepare yourself before a sandboarding tournament?

"I did training this winter and last winter, in the snow because I live in France; I did the Giant X tour in Switzerland; I did a long trip in Namibia as well for training."

- What's your favourite place for Sandboarding?

"After my trip in Namibia, definitely Namibia; because the landscape is just crazy, amazing; the dunes are really big."

- Do you think Cabo Verde will get more exposure for Sandboarding after your world cup win?

"I don't think so, the tourism isn't big enough for sandboarding. For people who want to discover something, it can be a good experience."

- How did you handle coming second in the slalom?

"Actually, it was surprising for me; because, slalom isn't my speciality; I was relaxed for the slalom because I already won the boardercross and I wanted to live the

experience, Luca Flachenecker was really strong and really fast and I couldn't win but second place is a good position, I'm happy with it."

- Do you have any messages for anyone who wants to get into Sandboarding?

"Just try and you'll fall in love, if you try sandboarding, you will want to go back on sand for sure; we have no seasons, you can try all year round!"

- What plans do you have in the next world cup?

"For the next world cup, I will do the same but the level is going up; I have to train more, the new generation is coming and they're training all year round, especially the Peruvians & Chileans; so it'll be hard for sure!"

Lon Beale

As the owner of a Sandboarding Park in the USA and as a keen sandboarder from an early age, Lon Beale is a cemented name in the sandboarding industry. Lon Beale is a veteran of the sandboarding scene, but some also credit him as the inventor of the Sandboard;

(Travelwithigor, 2016), and he was once the head of Dune Riders International. So if Cristiano Ronaldo is the titan of the football universe, Lon Beale is most definitely a titan for Sandboarding.

- What was it about Sandboarding that got you into the sport?

"I started in 1972 as I grew up in the Mojave Desert and visited the local dunes often. We tried different things to slide each time."

- What made you want to do more to promote and eventually expand the sport to more people?

"Probably the same motivation you have for doing your sandboarding book. A chance to share something cool with others. I come from a very progressive, generous family so sharing all we have is our way."

- What would you say is your best achievement since you started your sandboarding career?

"Sandboard Magazine (Sandboard.com) and Sand Master Park. They were both huge boosts toward giving birth to this sport and making it available to the public."

- Is there any one moment no matter how trivial during your sandboarding journey that you wish you done differently?

"*I would have liked to know more and had faith in the internet sooner. It's really the tool that brought sandboarding to the world. I am told over and over again that a group of individuals got into sandboarding because of Sandboard.com (1995) It took me a while to realize the full potential of the internet.*"

- How close do you think we are to seeing Sandboarding as a sport in sports tournaments such as the Olympics?

"*We were approached by the X-Games in 1997 but the sport was not available enough to be realistic. Bringing sandboarding into the Olympics will have to be someone else's project. We are much more involved with the recreational aspects of the sport these days.*"

- What do you think would encourage more people to take part in the sport?

"*At this point we see more and more people getting interested in sandboarding. It's steadily growing anyway but I think solid celebrity endorsements, TV series, or *featured in movies would create a rush on the sport as well."*

- What are your plans for the future of Sand Master Park?

"Sand Master Park has a good piece of prime property to cater to this sport. We fully intend to expand more than double our current store size with more offering to our visitors as well."

- What message would you want to give to people who are getting involved in the sport for the very first time?

"I would simply offer a sincere welcome to any and all who want to get into sandboarding. There is plenty of sand for everyone!"

Gabriel Cruz

Gabriel "Gabe" Cruz is a Sandboarding regular and instructor at Sand Master Park; he also happens to be a 3x world champion of Sandboarding. He was born and bred in the State of Oregon and has firmly established himself as one of the best Sandboarding athletes in the world.

- How did you discover sandboarding?

"I been boarding since I was 10 busy Sandboarding since I was 15. First boss that was also a good family friend I worked for had a few in his garage and he was going to take his son and my Lil bro Jackson out to the dunes. He threw a board my way and invited me out too!"

- What was it about Sandboarding that got you into the sport?

"It was new and different from what I was used to so I had to figure it out. It was fun and the dunes were a whole new world to me."

- How does it feel knowing you're a 3 time world champion?

"Being a champion is cool but really I'm still a normal guy!"

- What would you say is your best achievement since you started your sandboarding career?

"Being able to travel and see parts of the world I would have never seen before."

- Is there any one moment no matter how trivial during your sandboarding journey that you wish you done differently?

"Rode harder gone bigger traveled more done more"

- How would you prepare yourself before a sandboarding tournament?

"Listen to some good tunes something loud hard hitting and fast paced!"

- Do you have any career rivals?

"No rivals but it's always a good comp when my bro Jackson comes to town"

- What are your plans for the future of your sandboarding career?

"Teach my 3 month old daughter how to get ride a Sandboard now!"

- What message would you want to give to people who look up to you and what you've accomplished?

"Never give up! Competition gets tuff throw it bigger and harder then then! The only limits is what you put on yourself!"

Jamie Perkins

If you look up Sandboarding on YouTube, you'll find a video from Jamie Perkins as the first result; Jamie has been a YouTube user since 2006 and has bagged himself 2 million subscribers and racked up over 21 million views. The video "Sand Boarding In The Desert of Dubai" shows Perkins' experience in the United Arab Emirates and his time doing Sandboarding there. I got in touch with him, and even though he's only been Sandboarding once, I thought I'd ask him some questions:

- How did you first come across Sandboarding?

"I had seen a couple of people on YouTube Sand boarding and always thought it looked like a lot of fun so when I knew I was heading to the desert in Dubai, I did a bit of research and found a company who could provide the experience for me. It was a lot of fun!"

- Why did you end up going to the United Arab Emirates in particular?

"I've been to Dubai a bunch of times. Whenever I'm doing a stop over there I always make a point to spend a couple of days there. It's a really fun city but this particular trip was one with the tourism board of Dubai. They asked me to provide them with a bucket list worth of activities that I wanted to do in Dubai and they really delivered. It was one of the most fun and action packed weeks of my life. I did everything from racing a Porsche, drove boats, went to a water park, drove dune buggies, and a whole lot more. It was a great trip and I made a lot of really cool videos out of it too."

- What do you normally do when you travel abroad?

"When I'm traveling I always seek out unique experiences. I'm always looking to do something I've never done before. I also like to try local food and meet new people."

- What made you want to try out the sport?

"I'd seen some cool videos on YouTube. It looked like a lot of fun and it really was!"

- I notice that you're an Australian YouTuber and Australia has some well-known Sandboarding locations (one of the most notable being Kangaroo Island, South Australia) would you consider visiting them as well?

"Kangaroo Island is somewhere I've always wanted to visit. I didn't actually know it was a Sandboarding hot spot but now I know, I'll definitely try Sandboarding there when I eventually visit."

- Have your fans and followers seen your time on the sand dunes and reach out to you to say they tried it themselves?

"Yeah, I've had a bunch of people mention they've done it before and loved it since I posted that video."

- What benefits do you see in vlogging about your experiences when you do these type of activities?

"I really get a kick out of filming my experiences in an immersive way in hopes that I can share some of the excitement I felt at the time with other people. It's great to look back on these videos as a way to relive the experiences. It's also a great perk this actually being my job. Over the years I've been lucky enough to do some pretty amazing things that I can't imagine I would have been able to do had I worked in a different kind of career."

- Considering you've only been Sandboarding once, would you want to do it again?

"Most definitely! It's been a while since I did it but I'd love to give it another go."

Best Places For Sandboarding

I have been to several places in my time, and there are some magnificent sights when it comes to riding the sands; despite what people say that Sandboarding is a desert sport, there are also beaches and places near urban hot spots where the sport is thriving!

There are places on this list that I have not been to, but the good thing is about running a blog for eight years is that you know what to look for when you have access to an abundance of information. From the very start, I made a top 10 list of Sandboarding Nations on my blog. It did what it said on the tin, it ranked the best countries for Sandboarding, and I did this because I wanted to give my readers an indication of some of the best places to go as sporting tourists. The best website I used to help influence my decisions when making my top 10 lists was Numbeo.com which defines itself as "*the world's largest cost of living database*" and a "*crowd-sourced global database of quality of life informations including housing indicators, perceived crime rates, and quality of healthcare, among many other statistics."* (Numbeo.com, n.d.)

I gave each country a score based on the cost of living, quality of life, health care, crime rate, internet speeds, and whether their country is perceived as "Happy" on the World Happiness Report. Making a comprehensive list of all Sandboarding countries and listing all of their dunes for us Sandboarders sounds like a book of its own, so that I won't do here. However, I'll give some well-known places on the six continents of the world; Antarctica shall not feature on this list for obvious reasons. Although the sites I've included are my opinions, and it's a tough job as I have only limited myself to 6 on each continent, I'm sure I'll insert other sites if I publish a follow-up book in the future.

North America

As we will prove, Sandboarding doesn't happen in just the rocky and dusty deserts. Still, I'll admit the majority of the most famous dunes are in the United States, where most of the dusty deserts of North America are, and I'll do my best to include some from other countries as well. Although, as we'll discover, it won't just be all below Canada, and it won't be entirely on the continental mainland, there are plenty of places for practising on prized dunes, and North America sure has prized dunes.

- On the West Coast of the U.S., you've got Sand Master Park on Oregon Highway 101, which I've mentioned in this book too many times already; this place has a range of Beginner, Intermediate, and Expert slopes. Sand Master Park has lots of ramps and rails to ride on, which breaks the mould that you go down a dune or jump all the time to get an adrenaline boost. Unfortunately, this park doesn't have any lifts to take you to the top, yet not many places do.

"Oregon Dunes (Florence, Oregon, USA) 19" by James St. John is licensed under CC BY 2.0

- Going a little east of Kanab, Utah, lies the Coral Pink Sand Dunes State Park, which isn't too far from the border with Arizona. The most striking feature of these dunes is that they, in some places, are a very light shade of orange with a pinch of pink. Although these dunes regularly see hiking and off-roading, not all dunes are accessible as part of the park is a nature reserve, the day-use fee is $10 per vehicle, and camping is as little as $25 (Utah State Parks, n.d.)

"Coral Pink Sand Dunes 1989 01" by LBM1948 is licensed under CC BY-SA 4.0.

- I could go on with the rest of the Western United States, but I'll end it here for now and move to the East Coast where you find Jockey's Ridge State Park in Nags Head, North Carolina; not too far from Kitty Hawk, where the Wright Brothers' famously made their famous flight in 1903. Known as: "*A premier location for kites, sightseeing and sunsets, with a view arcing from the ocean to Roanoke Sound.*" (North Carolina State Parks, n.d.) This dune is well known for its hang gliding and offers Sandboarding lessons to individuals; there are businesses nearby that will happily lend you a Sandboard if you don't have one of your own.

"Jockey's Ridge State Park Nags Head 33" by Bohemian Baltimore is licensed under CC BY-SA 4.0

- Going North to Canada now, we go to the Carcross Desert; you read right, a desert in Canada. Several sources have considered this place the 'World's Smallest Desert' in the Yukon Territory. The dunes may be small, but these dunes are a hot spot for Sandboarding in the far north used all year round by sports and recreation enthusiasts; but in 1992, the Government of Yukon: "*sought environmental protection for the dunes but encountered some opposition from community members who use the area for recreation.*" (A.N., n.d.)

"Carcross Desert (1)" by Richard Martin is licensed under CC BY 2.0

- Taking a trip to Central America, we end up in Nicaragua, where you can have your ideal opportunity to Sandboard down an active volcano, and instead of fine sand, you will be surfing down a mixture of hardened lava and volcanic ashes; the last eruption occurred here in August 1999 and according to Sand-boarding.com: the latest eruption "*Gave birth to a slope of now hardened lava which made Sandboarding on Cerro Negro possible.*" (Sand-boarding.com, 2020) Also, Volcanoes are hazardous, so I'd highly advise getting insurance and listening to the instructors if you want to do this.

"Cerro Negro Volcano - Near Leon - Nicaragua - 06 (31609315435)" by Adam Jones is licensed under CC BY-SA 2.0

- Hopping off the Continent for a moment and going into the Caribbean, we find the Bani Dunes in the

Dominican Republic, where I'll be ending the North American section of this Chapter. If you're talking about the country as a whole, Jade Adele from We Travel And Blog puts it well: *"The Dominican Republic is like a little mini continent with nine different ecological zones, from pine forest mountain peaks, to mangrove shores, lush tropical jungles, and yes, even a desert!"* (Adele, J. n.d.) These dunes are 65km southwest of the nation's capital Santo Domingo, so they're not that remote from a large city; the dunes are on the coast, so I would imagine the climate won't be as harsh with that sea breeze. Admittedly, these dunes aren't as tall as ones on the North American mainland, but dunes as good as these are a rarity on the Caribbean Islands, so it's worth having a look.

"Dunas de Baní y sus costas" by Ronny Medina is licensed under CC BY-SA 4.0

South America

A common stereotype is that South America is associated with the Amazon rainforest or high altitude, rocky mountains. However, I can prove right here that Sandboarding is bustling and a sport that's commonplace here; out of all the continents where Sandboarding takes place, I'd have to admit I think the most enthusiasm and participation occurs in South America. And now here are some of the dunes:

- Our South American journey begins in Brazil, the largest country on the continent. One popular destination for all kinds of sporting tourists is the Lençóis Maranhenses National Park, where endless freshwater lagoons seemingly engulf the vast volume of dunes. The temperature of the park tends to stay the same all year round at a hot 28.5 degrees. (Miranda, J.P. 2012) and for any movie buffs reading, 2 of the 'Avengers' films were shot here; so if you're a film fan, this alone is an excellent reason to visit.

"Lençóis Maranhenses. 01" by LBM1948 is licensed under CC BY-SA 4.0

- We are staying in Brazil for a moment, but going much further south to Santa Catarina and the east of its state capital, Florianopolis. The city lies on the aptly named Santa Catarina Island, and the south of the island, you'll see the very impressive and diverse Dunas da Joaquina, and on the north of the island, you'll see the much smaller dunes on Santinho Beach. Tourists and locals flock here in droves to brush up on their skills, but sadly, the dunes are encroaching onto local houses and *"several homes have developed severe structural damage, and officials have declared the houses uninhabitable due to fears that their roofs could soon collapse."* (Rosenthal, Z. 2021)

"Florianopolis-dunes" by Rsabbatini is licensed under CC BY-SA 2.5

- We are leaving Brazil and paying our attention to the second smallest country on the continent, the first to legalise marijuana and the first location to host the Men's FIFA World Cup. Uruguay gets an honourable mention here due to its relatively inexpensive cost of living and declining crime rate; the dunes here are the ones at Cabo Polonio National Park. Probably the most curious fact about this place is that no roads are leading to the coastal hamlet, no electricity in the village except for the lighthouse, and no running water. "*the only way of visiting Cabo Polonio is by walking at least 7 kilometres or taking one of the official 4×4 trucks in.*" (Mowgli Adventures, 2021) These qualities don't make Cabo Polonio a rural backwater, more of a place with authentic originality.

"Dunas de Cabo Polonio" by Luciacasanovascasso is licensed under CC BY-SA 3.0

- Now it's time to pay a visit to the longest country in the world, Chile. I'll be looking at two places here, just like I did with Brazil; the first location in Chile is not too far from Valparaíso; I present to you the

Dunas de Concon. Atop the impressive dunes that sit near Valparaíso, your eyes gaze with a view that lets you see out beyond the Pacific coast and the city below. You'll find that you'll most likely be able to see the coastline from the summit of the dunes. In addition, there is a store where you can rent boards and buy waxes at the bottom of the dune. (Amor For Travel, 2018)

"Dunas De Concón (40046667682)" by Deensel is licensed under CC BY 2.0

- The second dune spot in Chile I'll mention here is in the northern city of Iquique. It is home to the Cerro Dragon or Dragon Hill with a length of 4 kilometres and a height of anywhere up to 500 metres; it makes Cerro Dragon *"the largest urban sand dune in the world."* (Patowary, K. 2014) According to the same article, the city residents are using this place to dump their refuse despite this dune being a hot spot for sports enthusiasts, particularly paragliders and, of course, sandboarders. You also get the view of the Pacific Ocean and the city below the summit from the top of the Dragon Hill, but given how high up it is, I wouldn't want to walk this!

"Iquique" by Pablo Trincado" is licensed under CC BY 2.0

- Our final stop on this continent is probably one of the most well known and infamous sandboarding locations on the map, hosting the Sandboard World Cup; it's Huacachina in Peru. The oasis in this village is visible on the 50 Sol banknote; sandboarding is so popular here countless stores are willing to rent boards and equipment to adrenaline-junkies like us; according to Sand-boarding.com: "*The Huacachina sand dunes reach heights up to 500 metres (1640 feet), as big as mountains (but not nearly as huge as the nearby Cerro Blanco, one of the tallest sand dunes in the world)."* (Sand-boarding.com, 2020) Cerro Blanco is in the same state as the dunes in Huacachina so that you could scale and ride down the dunes in Huacachina and Cerro Blanco in a day trip.

"Llacuna de l'oasi de Huacachina13" by Pitxiquin is licensed under CC BY-SA 4.0

Europe

Europe is the continent I call my home, and I will admit there isn't a lot of Sandboarding going on here, but if you venture out to the coasts or find a decent dune inland, you'll be presented with exciting places to try out Sandboarding. In terms of infrastructure, the continent tends to be very well connected. As towns and cities are relatively close together, there's no fear of being isolated or without basic amenities compared to the other continents.

- First up, my home country; the United Kingdom. There aren't that many dunes here for a modest-sized island. However, you have plenty of choices for Sandboarding on the coast, including many beaches and seaside towns such as Balmedie and Holywell Bay. My top location in the United Kingdom is Merthyr Mawr in South Wales; the tallest dune here is "The Big Dipper", known as *"the second largest dune in Europe."* (Morris, H. 2017) This dune has the honour of being the closest sandboarding location to my house, and once you get in the car park, the dune isn't a five or 10-minute walk; you can see it as you arrive. But, unfortunately, you don't have any shops nearby, just some toilets, and Candleston Castle that's been withered over the centuries.

"Big Dipper at Merthyr Mawr" by Jack Soley is licensed under CC BY-SA 4.0

- Crossing the channel and going to France, I've been to this next dune for some training in the past; It's an hour's drive from Bordeaux, and it's called the Dune of Pilat. The Big Dipper in Wales was the second largest dune in Europe, and the Dune of Pilat is the first, measuring at 3 kilometres across and with a width of 500 metres, it's between "*100 and 115 metres tall depending on the year.*" (France-voyage, n.d.) It has refreshments for sale during the day and a fair parking price. Indeed an excellent reason to travel here. However, a fellow Sandboarder once told me that Sandboarding is off-limits on the side facing the forest. So I decided to be a rebel, and at night-time, I sandboarded down the forest side; I haven't found any sources that say it's illegal or forbidden whether it's day or night, I wouldn't suggest you do it because if you do and get caught, it's your fault.

"Dune du Pilat - coté terre 2" by Tangopaso is a public domain work.

- Venturing off the continent for a moment, we go to the Canary Islands, specifically Gran Canaria and the resort of Maspalomas. The dunes are very clean and well preserved; the sand from the Sahara Desert is carried here in the trade winds every year. In addition, 400 hectares of the dunes are a designated nature reserve. (Hello Canary Islands, n.d.) Some companies and tour agencies in the area of Playa Del Inglés will take you for lessons and tours on the dunes, and after the session, you can always ride the camels across the dunes.

"GC Dunas de Maspalomas R08" by Marc Ryckaert is licensed under CC BY 3.0

- After seeing all the dunes near the coast in Europe, we are now approaching what appears to be the elephant in the room, Monte Kaolino in Bavaria, Germany. It's not on the coast, and as the crow flies, it's closer to Prague, capital of the Czech Republic, than the shoreline. Kaolinite was once mined here since the 19th century, and it wasn't until the 1950s, when the pile of quartz sand got so tall, a ski club opened. Monte Kaolino is one of the only dunes in the world that comes with a lift, which means for a price, you won't need to hike to the top; to top it all off: *"Monte Kaolino is also home to the Sandboarding World Championships, in which many of the same types of winter boarding competitions are held, but on sand. Speeds of up to 60 mph have been clocked."* (Atlas Obscura, n.d.)

"Seilbahn Monte Kaolino1" by Zonk43 is a public domain work.

- I only knew about this next dune as I was writing this chapter as I did my research, and before this chapter, I didn't even know this country had dunes or even Sandboarding. Salir Do Porto in Portugal. Sandboarding.com claims that: "*There is a majestic white sand dune of around 50m of height, where sandboarding and sand sledding are popular.*

The area surrounding the dune is well-maintained, with parking lots, bars, and recreational facilities." (Sand-boarding.com, 2020) Salir Do Porto is only a few hours drive from the country's two major cities of Lisbon and Porto. Not only are these dunes adequately maintained, but they also have plenty of bars, restaurants, and facilities nearby to accommodate tourists.

"Dunas de Salir do Porto - Portugal (3497800536)" by Vitor Oliveira is licensed under CC BY-SA 2.0

- Last but not least, my final European sandboarding location in Denmark. It debuted at number 1 in my "Top 10 Sandboarding Countries" list for 2020. Mainland Denmark isn't big, and despite its latitude, it still hosts some impressive dunes waiting to be exploited by keen sandboarders. The place I'm recommending has the name "Rubjerg Knude"; when in the year 1900, a lighthouse activated for the first time, but due to the shifting sands in the area, the lighthouse "*has been perched on a sand dune on the northern Danish coast, but coastal erosion from North Sea winds threatened to topple it into the sea.*" (BBC, 2019). The lighthouse that once watched the seas of the Skagerrak is now surrounded by shifting sands on all sides. Of course, the lighthouse only stands at 23 metres, and the dunes aren't far from that height but considering it's in a nation so far north, it's an oddity that makes a trip here worth it.

"Rubjerg Knude Fyr 2015" by Jörg Braukmann is licensed under CC BY-SA 4.0

Asia

Our sport needs one necessity to work; sand, and lots of it. Although thankfully, many deserts in the Middle East contain many dunes, so the majority of the nations here will be in that region. I'll include some countries in South & East Asia to keep this list varied to an extent; the continent is developing at an exponential rate, and with the ever-increasing tourism here, it's no wonder why Sandboarding in Asia has skyrocketed over the past few years. It isn't just the Arabian Peninsula that's experiencing this uptake in the sport; it's all across Asia.

- The first country I'll start this section of Asia is Israel; it's in a hostile region of the world surrounded by foes; given its location, and despite what you might have heard about the country, it's a modern progressive nation, with its prosperous tech industry. Israel is a pioneer in desalinisation, and the city of Tel Aviv attracts attention as one of the most gay-friendly cities globally (Kantor, L. 2019). There are some places here that are fit for a sandboarder. One of them is the middle of the desert; the Negev Desert is a region in Southern Israel attracting tourists here for decades. A tour company I can personally recommend here is Dror Bamidbar; they offer private tours and sandboarding lessons; you don't even need the experience to get involved.

"Complex Ripples in Sand Dune in Negev Desert" by Hezi Yizhaq is licensed under CC BY 3.0

- Separated by a few countries on the world map, we make our way into Saudi Arabia. I don't need to stress that this place has a lot of deserts; a large portion of the country is home to the "Rub' Al Khali" or Empty Quarter. There have been sweeping social and economic reforms in this country since Crown Prince Mohammed Bin Salman took control, there are so many places to choose from if you decide to have an adventurous trip here, and sadly I can't pick one. However, I will make an honourable mention to the dunes outside of Riyadh and the ones in Thumamah National Park; tourists flock here in droves to hire quad bikes and cross the dunes, and have picnics, so why not bring your board and harness the potential that this park has to offer.

"Rub al Khali 002" by Nepenthes is licensed under CC BY-SA 3.0

- Qatar is my final stop in the Middle East region, where the 2022 FIFA World Cup will commence and where ever-increasing numbers of people are choosing to visit. These dunes have a unique quality, like the Pink Sand Dunes in Utah; the dunes I'm about to talk about make noises. Really. The Singing Sand Dunes just South of Doha *are an approximately 100 square km area with about 60 meter high sand dunes which create a magical vibrating sound when you move the sand. Some call it singing or humming, others farting."* (Off Beat Qatar, n.d.) Near the dunes, there are no restrooms, food stores, petrol stations, or places nearby to charge phones, so bring all your provisions you'll need for a great day out before you leave; and as with anywhere in this part of the world: wear a wide hat and put on sunblock.

"Singing sand dunes" by Peter is licensed under CC BY 2.0

- I've had the opportunity to travel to this following country back in 2017; it wasn't for a Sandboarding trip, sadly. India, however, does have dunes to offer to keen Sandboarders looking to score some Sandboarding, specifically in Rajasthan and the Thar Desert. There are many dunes in-between the two cities of Jodhpur and Jaisalmer; according to Rajasthan Yatra: "*The main locations where you will find sand dunes are Sam Village, Khuri Village, Ludharwa, Kanoi and Kuldhara.*" (Rajasthan Yatra, n.d.) I can't pinpoint one place as I haven't personally heard of any Sandboarding experiences in India. Still, I would suspect that many places in Rajasthan state or indeed the Thar Desert would accommodate the Sandboarding nation.

"Sand dunes of Rajasthan India" by Sumeet Jain is licensed under CC BY-SA 2.0

- Going north towards the 3rd largest country globally, China, it's a big country. Therefore, China naturally has a lot of landscapes: deserts, tundra, plains, steppe, and the vast towns and cities that have undergone expansion in recent years. A well-known place for hitting the dunes is in Kumtag Desert, most notably Mingsha Mountain, also known as the Singing Sand Dunes (not to be confused with the Singing Sand Dunes in Qatar) Dunhuang in North-western China. The best advice on visiting the region according to Top China Travel is as follows: "*May to October is the best time to visit Crescent Spring. Visiting Singing Sand Dune, the best time should be afternoon and toward evening. Recommended tourists who want to visit Dunhuang avoid winter vacation, during this time the average temperature of Dunhuang would be 9.3 degree below zero, the day and night temperate difference is quite large, therefore it is not suitable to travel during winter."* (Top China Travel, n.d.) As China is a vast country and the local airport is approximately 10 kilometres away, you'll most definitely get satisfaction from visiting this site.

"Crescent Moon Spring Yueyaquan Mingshashan Dunhuang Gansu China 敦煌 鸣沙山 月牙泉 - panoramio (2)" by Hiroki Ogawa is licensed under CC BY 3.0

- And our last stop in Asia is off the continent but still in the Far East; it's Japan. Japan is known for being a futuristic society and for having unique customs and traditions you wouldn't find anywhere else on the planet. For example, Japan hosts the Tottori Sand Dunes for us sandboarders. There is a paragliding school for those who wish to explore the sky. For those who prefer land, there's a Sandboarding school. Finally, for those who like the land but wish to do neither, you can also hire a camel ride across the dunes. "*The dunes have splendid 30-degree slopes that are not too difficult for beginners to tackle nor too easy for experienced boarders to show off their tricks.*"(Koolen, B. 2017) Tottori Station is a 10-minute drive from the dunes, so if you're not looking to have a long hike or spend a lot on taxis, this might be up your street.

"Tottori-Sakyu Tottori Japan" by Hashi photo is licensed under CC BY-SA 1.0

Africa

Africa is home to the world's largest desert, with many cultures, languages, ethnic groups, religions, and traditions that make this place one of a kind. Unfortunately, there aren't many desert areas outside the Sahara and Kalahari. Still, there are entrepreneurs taking advantage of the dunes and driving up tourism in the regions that do contain desert. As a result, sandboarding is becoming a sport on the bucket list for many people who travel to Africa. Tourism is changing the lives of the people who operate tours and Sandboarding schools, boosting the economy and improving the livelihoods of the communities near these dunes.

- Our first stop is the very bottom of the continent in South Africa; while there are plenty of coastal dunes and the many sports tourists who come here for Sandboarding, they will end up near the border with Namibia, Cape Town, or Mossel Bay. So instead, I'll be paying attention to the Atlantis Sand Dunes, just under an hours' drive from Cape Town. These dunes cover an area of 32 square kilometres (12.4 square miles); it's worth mentioning that according to Cape Town's travel website: *"Atlantis is more than a centre for adventure sports, it makes for some amazing photo opportunities with its ever-changing landscape of pure white sand dunes reaching up to 50 metres (160 feet) high. The dunes are a haven for sandboarding, quad biking, extreme 4×4 rides and self-drive dune tours, and off-roading. The area is also frequented by film crews, and the landscape appears in countless movies and adverts."* (Cape Town Tourism, n.d.)

If you visit Cape Town, it looks as if hitting the dunes might be a good day out.

"Ladybird Sandboarding Boarding" by Bongani2 is licensed under CC BY-SA 3.0

- Going further North-west on the map, we end up in the home of the Kalahari & Namib deserts; that nation is Namibia. Namibia was the first destination in the Simon Reeve documentary series shown on the BBC, Tropic of Capricorn, where he tried out Sandboarding. People into Sandboarding can identify into one of two categories, those who want to go to

Namibia and those who've already been. Namibia is probably the most well-known country for Sandboarding, and there are many pilgrimages to Walvis Bay, Swakopmund, and Sossusvlei. However, Namibia is one of the countries where it's hard to focus my attention on one area. This place contains so much diversity and is therefore often praised as a sanctuary for many Sandboarders. As National Geographic puts it: *"For sandboarding fans, the call of the dunes on the outskirts of town is strong. While Sossusvlei's slopes may be three times as high, Swakopmund's are steep enough to give you plenty of acceleration. It's a long climb to the top, but the buzz as you hurtle down, either standing up or lying down, is worth every step."* (Gregg, E. 2021)

"Sandboarding, Namibia (20629430364)" by Luke Price is licensed under CC BY 2.0

- Staying in Southern Africa, we'll visit our final stop in this region of the continent. Mozambique is one of the few Portuguese-speaking countries on the continent, and despite not having any desert areas, it contains spectacular beach dunes, notably on Bazaruto Island. It's a beautiful spot when you consider that there are horses and reefs on and around the islands; there's a lot of angling in the area as well. Mozambique is another place I didn't know about before writing this book, and I also didn't know that Mozambique is a popular tourist destination well-known for its beaches; Joss Kent, the CEO of

AndBeyond, explained Mozambique well:
"*Mozambique offers travelers a balmy climate, miles of untouched beaches and colorful Portuguese and Arabic heritage. Add to this the warm and friendly people, incredible cuisine, based heavily on abundant seafood and fiery spices. It's what has made and strongly continues to make Mozambique an irresistible and authentic African beach experience.*" (Reinstein, D. 2019)

"Bazaruto-Island-East-Coast-From-South" by Bjørn Christian Tørrissen is licensed under CC BY-SA 3.0

- Going to the very top of Africa and heading to the world's largest hot desert, our first stop is one of the cradles of civilisation, Egypt. It's home to a large portion of desert, pyramids and has one of the most notable Sandboarding scenes outside of the Americas. In Egypt, there exist plenty of entrepreneurs and companies that'll take you off-roading and surfing down the dunes and will even provide you with the latest equipment to help you grind the dunes in one of the most cultural and historical places on earth. As I said earlier in this book, there's not much evidence to support that Sandboarding indeed originated here as no hieroglyphics depicted the sport. Still, it's understandable that people think that due to the sheer volume of dunes here. Outside of the Cairo & Nile areas, you'll find the White Desert & the Black Desert; the Black Desert, for instance: *"features a myriad of unique mountain ranges. Each one carries a coat of black stones thrown out of volcanoes millions of years ago, giving the sandy landscape its colored name."* (Boraie, E. 2020) So despite having a desert and sandy landscape covering most of the nation, it's not all the same old desert.

"Sandboarding at El Safra dune in Sinai" by Trekkingsinai is licensed under CC BY-SA 3.0

- Going a little west, crossing Libya, we find ourselves in tiny Tunisia, the northernmost country on the African continent. Tunisia is somewhat personally remarkable as its independence day happens to be on my birthday. My focal point for this country is the island of Djerba. Many know this place for the home of Tatooine in the Star Wars series, but this place is home to Sandboarding potential as many people come to Djerba for Sandboarding and see the famous film set. As recently as 2021, to mark "National Sports

Press Day", it was reported that a conference to boost the potential for sports tourism in the country commenced: "*The conference will discuss the opportunities offered by sports events to promote tourism and ways to boost cooperation with sports federations and governmental and private structures in charge of tourism, in order to increase the number of international sports events in Tunisia.*" (Tunis Afrique Presse, 2021) This conference, in my view, could potentially pave the way for more sports to take place here, not just sports with large audiences such as football and Olympic events but hopefully niche sports such as Sandboarding as well.

"Tunisia-3694 - One BIG Sandbox........ (8024778458)" by Dennis Jarvis is licensed under CC BY-SA 2.0

- Our final location is still in the North of Africa, Algeria. Algeria since 2011 has been the largest country by area in Africa. While it doesn't receive as much tourism as its neighbour to the west or in the Arab World as a whole, it is one of these countries where you can't find the best dunes in one location. Honourable mentions here include the Issaouane Erg, which covers almost 40,000 square kilometres in the East of the country and the town of Taghit, which run alongside the Grand Erg Occidental. Unsurprisingly, Taghit is: "*The best place in Algeria to go sandboarding or skiing down the massive Saharan sand dunes that stretches out for more than 600km from here, a place which is also a perfect place to go Quadbike driving or camel riding in the desert.*" (L, Christian. 2020) Algeria, as it seems, is huge, and so are its opportunities.

"Taghit 4" by LBM1948 is licensed under CC BY-SA 4.0

Oceania

Oceania is our final continent on this voyage, searching for the world's best sandboarding destinations. It's probably no surprise that we'll most likely end up in the most populated and largest nations in the area; Australia and New Zealand. Luckily, I managed to find other destinations elsewhere in the region that would make an excellent place to hit the dunes as well if you're in the area.

Most, if not all, of the Sandboarding in this part of the world occurs in Australia and New Zealand, so I made it my mission to find the best places for hitting the dunes in this part of the world.

- Our initial stop is in Western Australia, a town over 100 kilometres north of Perth; the small fishing and tourist town of Lancelin is also home to the Lancelin Sand Dunes, the largest in Western Australia. Lancelin has been blessed with 2 kilometres of dunes with no vegetation to stop you; this spot is also a top destination for those who prefer off-roading on what appears to be endless dunes. Aside from Sandboarding, this place is also a designated spot for kitesurfing, windsurfing, off-roading, and as it's on the coast; in addition, I would suspect that surfing would be typical. These dunes were also the location for a Guinness World Record, "*The largest convoy of off-road vehicles consisted of 449 vehicles and was organised by Lancelin District Community Association (Australia), on 15 October 2016.*" (Guinness World Records, n.d.)

"Lancelin Sand Dunes 2" by CyclonicallyDeranged is licensed under CC BY-SA 4.0

- Staying in Australia but heading to the South, we find the place with one of the most Australian sounding places in the world, Kangaroo Island in South Australia. The dunes on Kangaroo Island are best explored by either a sledge or sandboard, both available for hire. The dunes on Kangaroo Island are also known as the "Little Sahara", the sizes of the dunes vary across the dune system, but the highest dune is approximately 70 metres above sea level. Unlike most of the places I've covered in this part of the book, many people come here to witness unique wildlife such as koalas, seals, and Ligurian bees that call this island their home. *"The dunes are located on private property; however, the owner has graciously allowed tourists to enjoy the dunes. In the late 1970s, the Geological Society of Australia heritage listed Little Sahara as a geological monument, along with nineteen other sites on Kangaroo Island."* (Sightseeing Tours Australia, n.d.) I also learned that Australian Winter Olympians also train here, so if it's good enough for them, it sure would be good enough for us!

"Little Sahara (147321123)" by Deborah Pickett is licensed under CC BY 3.0

- As much as Australia has many dunes, I must leave this great nation and across the sea to another, New Zealand. Although many sports take place across the two islands, I'll start on the South Island; 15 kilometres east of Dunedin, the 7th largest city by population; Sandfly Bay, a quiet dune system coastal area on the Otago Peninsula. Like Kangaroo Island in Australia, the site is also a regular visiting spot for those who wish to see nature, specifically sea lions and penguins. Speaking of the beach for a moment: "*The beach is surrounded by sand dunes, cliffs and surging waves. People often play sports on the flat areas, while others ride down the sand dunes on old skateboards.*" (Phillips, R. n.d.) Aside from being a well-known hiking and rambling spot, not many other recreational activities are known here, and the dunes aren't that great compared to other places in this book. Still, I've included this destination here because of its isolation from the bulk of tourists that would otherwise visit the country.

"Sandfly bay May-2007" by Stug.stug is licensed under CC BY-SA 3.0

- Staying in New Zealand but changing Island, I give you what is undoubtedly the only worthy and most notorious Sandboarding spot in New Zealand, the Te Paki Sand Dunes at Cape Reinga. If you search for Sandboarding in New Zealand, this is your main result, and no other dune system in New Zealand will top this. If you want to know about the Geography of these dunes: *"The Te Paki sand dunes were once a part of their own island, separated from what is now mainland New Zealand. Over millions of years the narrow mass of land was pushed by sand buildup from volcanoes in the south, eventually shifting the lands to connection."* (Beddall, L. 2018) Te Paki Sand Dunes is a spectacular destination and is near the famous Ninety Mile Beach, but keep in mind that there are many injuries on these dunes and as recent as 2019, "*a 68-year-old from South Korea, had been on a tour bus, before he was struck by another bus on the same tour while he was boarding down a dune*" (Williams, C. 2019) The man in question, sadly died.

"Sand Surfing Te Paki Sand Dunes. (20219345235)" by Bernard Spragg is a public domain work.

- Onto the islands of Oceania, where we are well in the Pacific Ocean now; our next travel destination is the island nation of Fiji. It's understandable for thinking that these small Pacific Islands would lack dunes necessary for a good bit of Sandboarding. Still, if you travel to Sigatoka on the island of Viti Levu, you will find dunes. A lot of running happens on these dunes, particularly with rugby players who are training, there isn't too much documentation of Sandboarding on these dunes, but from one source, the dunes had the following description: "*The undulating dunes hug the territory for 5 km with their soft sand as fine as flour. The tops of these 20 to 60-metre sand hillocks afford a beautiful vista of green mountains to one side and the boundless ocean to the other.*" (Rove.me, 2019)

"[path of the dunes]" by Kyle Post is licensed under CC BY 2.0

- And last but by no means least in this extensive section of this book, our final sandboarding country we'll be paying a visit to in this book is Vanuatu, another Pacific Island country. The place I'll be including here is an outlier as it's a lot like Cerro Negro in Nicaragua, where it's a volcano; the difference is that as I write this, in the year 2022, the Mount Yasur volcano is still erupting and has been since at least 1774. (Volcano Discovery, n.d.) Despite the consistent eruption and the risk of death with flying lava bombs, you can find videos of people skiing and boarding down Mount Yasur. In the year 2002, Zoltan Istvan wrote about his experience volcano boarding down Mount Yasur: "*The smell of sulfur was intense, and thousands of hardened lava rocks grounded on the crater's edge distressed me. This was nature's war zone ... I hadn't gotten far when a second explosion shook the mountain. Thirty meters to my right, a huge lava bomb landed, broke into pieces, then tumbled down the slope. The greatest danger with volcano boarding is not being able to see where the mountain is shooting its molten entrails -- Russian roulette came to mind.*" (Istvan, Z. 2002) I wouldn't recommend doing this, it's a bit too volcanic for my liking, but I have to admit, it would be a once in a lifetime experience.

"Yasur (32012271358)" by David Stanley is licensed under CC BY 2.0

As I've illustrated already, I'm fully aware that there are many more places around the world where Sandboarding is a sport that's regularly practised. Still, by including this condensed list of 6 places per continent, it'll give you a rough idea of the places that I found intriguing and who knows, maybe I might write a follow-up book in the future with dunes from every country in the world. Of course, I cannot guarantee that these locations I've mentioned will allow Sandboarding in the future as rules can change at any time.

Sandboarding Bites

As part of my service of providing suitable places for Sandboarding: it's only good practise to give some handy tips regarding travel, etiquette, caring for your board, and performance, as well as other miscellaneous bits of advice that might be relevant for a specific situation. Therefore, I included small posts as tips and guidance under the name of "Sandboarding Bites", and I'll share them all, keep in mind some of these will be blindly obvious, but some others may be new to you.

- Before you go Sandboarding, it's always essential to check your weather forecast before you get there; there's nothing worse than wet weather ruining a good session on the dunes.

- If you're going down a dune at high speed, always slow down before a bend rather than during the descent, always try and lean your body back while you're on your board; raising your hands to slow you down should always be a last resort.

- If you have any excess sandboarding wax, don't throw it in the bin. You can sell your wax or even recycle it; if you're looking to use it again, keep it in a cool place so it doesn't go bad.

- A snowboard will still go down a sand dune; it will perform nowhere near as well as a conventional sandboard; but with a bit of sandboard wax, it's a great cheap alternative!

- Always clean your board regularly, a small piece of grit can cost you time and money if you don't take care of your board.

- Position is key; bend too little, you won't turn & bend too much, you'll fall in the sand and roll on your face.

- Sandboarding in the cold can be a good sport too, always keep hydrated because the air's drier and you'll use more energy heating your body.

- Appropriate footwear is key to a fun ride, heavy boots and high heels won't suffice; try some trainers, or even go with a pair of socks.

- Your eyes are precious, keep them working well and invest in some goggles; to stop sand entering the eye area, and from harmful UV rays.

- Don't throw away your old sunblock, some sun lotions can last up to a good 2 years once opened before it gets defective.

- Going abroad? Take out travel insurance before you leave, it'll save you a fortune in medical expenses.

- If where you are is quite remote and you can't get a phone signal, it's always a good idea to keep some spare change just in case you need to make an emergency call.

- If you're a European citizen travelling within the European Union, get a European Health Insurance Card along with your travel insurance so your national healthcare goes on holiday with you.

- If you're taking a vehicle with you to the dunes, always carry spare drinking water and a first aid kit. If you're in a rural spot and don't have access to water, some safe water purification tablets will work just as well.

- Always check expiry dates on Sandboarding waxes, they will be less effective over time.

- Looking for the ideal vehicle for the dunes? It's best to look for a 4-wheel drive and the highest amount of torque to tackle the steep dunes.

- Can you ride here? It's a good call to ask a local ranger, land owner, or a police officer before you can ride a dune.

- A lot of parks and dune regions will have parking spots, always check you're parked legally and if you need to, make sure you have enough money to pay the parking fee. It'll save you the embarrassment of getting a ticket on your car, and a lot of money from paying a fine!

- Some places are dangerous for travel, not because of war but disease; Some countries will require a certificate proving you've been vaccinated against certain illnesses, check with a medical professional and/or your country's foreign office before you travel.

- Are you travelling on an aircraft with your Sandboard? Airlines have different policies on their luggage, almost all airlines agree that your Sandboard will have to be declared as hold luggage. Don't assume that you can just use your board as part of your luggage allowance; Due to the nature of the awkward shape and dimensions of these boards, it's most likely that Sandboards will have to be 'Sports Equipment' which will cost you extra but it's good to check with airlines before you fly.

- Are you going somewhere where you've never been before? If the terrain or conditions aren't what you're used to; it may be worthwhile booking a session with a local instructor or sandboarding school, if you're fairly experienced on the dunes you won't need to have as many lessons as a beginner.

- Don't be impatient; if someone's already going down on the dune solo, wait for them to finish first.

- There's a common stereotype that the British prefer to talk slow and shout in English rather than make an effort in the local language, but if you want to make friends, do your best to converse in the local language.

- This one shouldn't apply to a lot of us but if you're going Sandboarding, don't leave your litter behind; either put it in the bins nearby or take it with you to dispose later. Littering makes the surrounding area worse for the locals, wildlife, and people who want to visit in the future.

Final Thoughts

I wrote this book merely as a tool to help those in the Sandboarding industry. I also wrote this as a guide to those who were curious or just getting started; I realised that there were no records in the British Library of any published books solely on Sandboarding. Some books that explored extreme sports briefly mention Sandboarding as a footnote or a chapter, but not as an entire book. I, therefore, decided to write the first Sandboarding book.

Ever since I first rode those dunes at Holywell Bay, I realised that I wanted to be a part of this sport, no matter how small the fan base or participation was. I'd always be happy to help with any expansion or development opportunities that Sandboarding would provide, not just to a potential career as an athlete but for the progress of this niche sport as a whole.

I hope this book gives everything you need to know about such topics as the qualities to possess if you're Sandboarding, what to look for when going out on a Sandboard, and how to be seen as a natural sandboarder.

As I said at the very start of this book, I want to claim that everything is to the best of my knowledge; all opinions and thoughts are my own unless otherwise referenced. I don't claim to be an expert in the field as I'm pretty sure other sportspeople have been in their chosen sport for longer than I have. The people I've spoken to and met in my journey since I started Sandboarding and when I started blogging have given me a unique perspective, welcomed my ideas, and generally are the most down-to-earth, understanding, and most genuine people you'll meet. I value what these people said and have done throughout the years.

If you've made it this far and you want to go out on the dunes, if you want to meet new people, if you're going to go on adventures, and if you're inspired to try something new; I'm grateful that I've encouraged you to want to do this. It's a fantastic thing to experience and be a part of; I appreciate you taking the time to read this book and take in the information I've put forward, it wasn't an easy job, but I feel good knowing I had done something worthwhile with my spare time.

My mission was to write an informative book on the sport that means the most to me, encourage more people to take part in the sport, and bring Sandboarding more into public knowledge; only time will tell, but I hope you think I did a good job.

References

Parcelforce Worldwide (n.d.) Why do Parcelforce Worldwide charge customs clearance fees. Retrieved from Parcelforce: https://www.parcelforce.com/help-and-advice/receiving/why-do-parcelforce-worldwide-charge-customs-clearance-fees (Accessed: 18th February 2020)

Dalia Research (2017) Made-In-Country-Index. Retrieved from Statista: https://www.statista.com/page/Made-In-Country-Index (Accessed: 18th February 2020)

Soley, J. (2019) Helmets for Sandboarding. Retrieved from Sandboarding Nation: www.sandboarding-nation.com/p/helmets-for-sandboarding/ (Accessed: 2nd January 2022)

Romantic Oregon Coast Vacations (n.d.) An Interview with Josh Tenge. Retrieved from Romantic Oregon Coast: http://www.romantic-oregon-coast.com/josh-tenge.html (Accessed: 2nd January 2022)

Soley, J. (2019) Who is Alex Bird? Retrieved from Sandboarding Nation: http://www.sandboarding-nation.com/2019/02/who-is-alex-bird.html (Accessed: 2nd January 2022)

Eleftheriou, D. (2012) Top 5 places for sandboarding. Retrieved from Surfdome: https://www.surfdome.com/blog/top-5-places-sandboarding (Accessed: 2nd January 2022)

Old Town Inn. (2019) Sandboarding in Florence: Everything You Need to Know. Retrieved from Old Town Inn: https://old-town-inn.com/sandboarding-in-florence/ (Accessed: 2nd January 2022)

Sandboard Magazine (n.d.) Who Invented Sandboarding? Retrieved from Sandboard Magazine: http://www.sandboard.com/drdune/ask/ask8.htm (Accessed: 9th February 2020)

Kissell, J. (2019) Sandboarding. Retrieved from Interesting Thing Of The Day: https://itotd.com/articles/6983/sandboarding/ (Accessed: 9th February 2020)

Actionhub Reporters (2017) An Introduction to Sandboarding. Retrieved from Actionhub: https://www.actionhub.com/stories/2017/02/14/an-introduction-to-sandboarding/ (Accessed: 9th February 2020)

Sengers, M. (2017) The Art of Sand Boarding. Retrieved from Twatours: https://www.twatours.com.au/single-post/2017/04/18/The-Art-of-Sand-Boarding (Accessed: 9th February 2020)

YourDictionary (n.d.) Sandboarding Meaning. Retrieved from YourDictionary: https://www.yourdictionary.com/sandboarding (Accessed: 2nd January 2022)

Dune Riders International (2021) Dune Riders International. Retrieved from Facebook: https://www.facebook.com/DuneRidersInternational/ (Accessed: 2nd January 2022)

Intersands (n.d.) Mision. Retrieved from Intersands: https://intersand.org/es/mision/ (Accessed: 17th October 2021)

Doody, P. (2019). Sand Dune - Country Report, Great Britain. Retrieved from Coastal Wiki: http://www.coastalwiki.org/wiki/Sand_dune_-_Country_Report,_Great_Britain (Accessed: 23rd October 2021)

U.S. Department of the Interior (n.d.) NPS Stats. Retrieved from National Park Service: https://irma.nps.gov/STATS/Reports/National (Accessed: 2nd January 2022)

Soley, J. (2020) The Trouble with Travel Insurance. Retrieved from Sandboarding Nation: https://www.sandboarding-nation.com/2020/01/the-trouble-with-travel-insurance.html/ (Accessed: 2nd January 2022)

Department for Transport (2019) 'Table RAS30001: Reported casualties by road user type, age and severity, Great Britain 2019'. Retrieved from The Royal Society for the Prevention of Accidents: https://rospa.com/road-safety/advice/cyclists-and-motorcyclists/accident-rates/ (Accessed: 2nd January 2022)

Persall, F. (n.d.) How Many People Die Skiing. Retrieved from Snowgaper: https://snowgaper.com/how-many-people-die-skiing/#injuries-per-year-for-skiers-and-snowboarders (Accessed: 31st October 2021)

Fone, M. (2019) Curious Questions: How likely are you to be killed by a falling coconut? Retrieved from Countrylife: https://www.countrylife.co.uk/comment-opinion/curious-questions-likely-killed-falling-coconut-207339 (Accessed: 31st October 2021)

Travelwithigor (2016) Sand Master Park - The Mecca of sandboarding. Retrieved from Travelwithigor: https://travelwithigor.wordpress.com/2016/06/29/sand-master-park-the-mecca-of-sandboarding/ (Accessed: 15th November 2021)

Numbeo (n.d.) Cost Of Living. Retrieved from Numbeo: https://www.numbeo.com/cost-of-living/ (Accessed: 29th November 2021)

Utah State Parks (n.d.) Park Fees. Retrieved from Utah State Parks: https://stateparks.utah.gov/parks/coral-pink/park-fees/ (Accessed: 6th December 2021)

North Carolina State Parks (n.d.) Jockeys Ridge State Park. Retrieved from North Carolina State Parks: https://www.ncparks.gov/jockeys-ridge-state-park/home (Accessed: 6th December 2021)

A.N. (n.d.) Carcross, Yukon. Retrieved from Canadian Geographic: http://www.canadiangeographic.ca/travel/travel_magazine/summer_2007/gateway_nature.asp (Accessed: 6th December 2021)

Sand-boarding.com (2020) Volcano surfing in Nicaragua (Cerro Negro Sandboarding). Retrieved from Sand-boarding: https://sand-boarding.com/volcano-boarding-in-nicaragua/ (Accessed: 6th December 2021)

Adele, J. (n.d.) Dunas de Bani Shenanigans. Retrieved from We Travel And Blog: https://wetravelandblog.com/2014/where-in-the-world/dunas-de-bani-shenanigans/ (Accessed: 6th December 2021)

Miranda, J.P. (2012) Reptiles from Lençóis Maranhenses National Park, Maranhão, northeastern Brazil. Retrieved from National Center of Biotechnology Information: https://www.ncbi.nlm.nih.gov/pmc/articles/PMC3520146/ (Accessed: 11th December 2021)

Rosenthal, Z. (2021) Gargantuan sand dunes 'swallow' oceanfront homes. Retrieved from Yahoo News: https://news.yahoo.com/gargantuan-sand-dunes-swallow-oceanfront-144551093.html (Accessed: 11th December 2021)

Mowgli Adventures (2021) How to get to Cabo Polonio. Retrieved from Mowgli Adventures: https://mowgli-adventures.com/how-to-get-to-cabo-polonio-uruguay/ (Accessed: 11th December 2021)

Amor For Travel (2018) Chile Sand Dunes of Concon An Unexpected Oasis. Retrieved from Amorfortravel: http://amorfortravel.com/chile-sand-dunes-concon-valparaiso/ (Accessed: 11th December 2021)

Patowary, K. (2014) The Dragon Hill of Iquique, Chile. Retrieved from Amusing Planet: https://www.amusingplanet.com/2014/10/the-dragon-hill-of-iquique-chile.html (Accessed: 11th December 2021)

Sand-boarding.com (2020) Sandboarding the Dunes of Huacachina Oasis in Peru. Retrieved from Sand-boarding:

https://sand-boarding.com/sandboarding-in-huacachina/ (Accessed: 11th December 2021)

Morris, H. (2017) The Welsh village that's the surprising home to Europe's second biggest sand dune. Retrieved from The Telegraph: https://www.telegraph.co.uk/travel/destinations/europe/united-kingdom/wales/articles/surprising-home-to-europe-second-largest-sand-dune-merthyr-mawr/ (Accessed: 13th December 2021)

France-voyage (n.d.) The Dune of Pilat. Retrieved from France-voyage: https://www.france-voyage.com/tourism/dune-pilat-364.htm (Accessed: 13th December 2021)

Hello Canary Islands (n.d.) Maspalomas Dunes Nature Reserve. Retrieved from Hello Canary Islands: https://www.hellocanaryislands.com/nature-spaces/gran-canaria/maspalomas-dunes-nature-reserve/ (Accessed: 13th December 2021)

Atlas Obscura (n.d.) Monte Kaolino - Hirschau, Germany. Retrieved from Atlas Obscura: https://www.atlasobscura.com/places/monte-kaolino (Accessed: 13th December 2021)

Sand-boarding.com (2020) Sandboarding at Salir do Porto. Retrieved from Sand-boarding: https://sand-boarding.com/forum/topic/sandboarding-at-salir-do-porto-portugal/ (Accessed: 13th December 2021)

BBC (2019) Danish Rubjerg lighthouse moved inland on skates. Retrieved from BBC: https://www.bbc.co.uk/news/world-europe-50139900 (Accessed: 13th December 2021)

Kantor, L. (2019) Why Tel Aviv Is One of the Most LGBTQ-Friendly Cities in the World. Retrieved from The Culture Trip: https://theculturetrip.com/middle-east/israel/articles/why-tel-aviv-is-one-of-the-most-lgbt-friendly-cities-in-the-world (Accessed: 14th December 2021)

Off Beat Qatar (n.d.) Singing Sand Dunes. Retrieved from Off Beat Qatar: https://www.offbeatqatar.com/place/singing-sand-dunes/ (Accessed: 14th December 2021)

Rajasthan Yatra (n.d.) Sand Dunes in Rajasthan. Retrieved from Rajasthan Yatra: https://rajasthanyatra.com/sand-dunes-in-rajasthan.html (Accessed: 14th December 2021)

Top China Travel (n.d.) Crescent Lake Dunhuang & Singing Sands Dune. Retrieved from Top China Travel: https://www.topchinatravel.com/china-attractions/misha-hill-and-crescent-spring.htm (Accessed: 14th December 2021)

Koolen, B. (2017) Desert Adventures: Visiting Japan's Tottori Sand Dunes. Retrieved from Japan Cheapo: https://japancheapo.com/entertainment/tottori-sand-dunes/ (Accessed: 14th December 2021)

Cape Town Travel (n.d.) The Atlantis Dunes: The Official Guide. Retrieved from Cape Town Tourism: https://www.capetown.travel/atlantis-dunes (Accessed: 20th December 2021)

Gregg, E. (2021) Eight ultimate adventures for every ability in Namibia. Retrieved from National Geographic:

https://www.nationalgeographic.co.uk/travel/2021/02/ultimate-adventures-namibia (Accessed: 20th December 2021)

Reinstein, D. (2019) Venturing Beyond the Beach in Mozambique. Retrieved from Travel Weekly: https://www.travelweekly.com/Middle-East-Africa-Travel/Venturing-beyond-the-beach-in-Mozambique (Accessed: 20th December 2021)

Boraie, E. (2020) Egypt's White Desert: The alien landscape beyond the Pyramids. Retrieved from CNN: https://edition.cnn.com/travel/article/egypt-white-desert/index.html (Accessed: 20th December 2021)

Tunis Afrique Presse (2021) National Sports Press Day: Promoting sports tourism to be debated at TAP's initative. Retrieved from Tunis Afrique Presse: https://www.tap.info.tn/en/Portal-Sports/14707216-national-sports (Accessed: 20th December 2021)

L, Christian. (2020) Taghit A Sahara Desert Oasis In Algeria. Retrieved from Unusual Traveler: https://www.unusualtraveler.com/taghit-a-sahara-desert-oasis-in-algeria/ (Accessed: 22nd December 2021)

Guinness World Records (n.d.) Largest convoy of off-road vehicles. Retrieved from Guinness World Records: https://www.guinnessworldrecords.com/world-records/99623-largest-convoy-of-off-road-vehicles (Accessed: 28th December 2021)

Sightseeing Tours Australia (n.d.) Little Sahara on Kangaroo Island. Retrieved from Sightseeing Tours Australia:

https://kangarooislandtoursaustralia.com.au/blog/little-sahara-on-kangaroo-island/ (Accessed: 28th December 2021)

Phillips, R. (n.d.) Sandfly Bay. Retrieved from Dunedin Attractions: https://dunedinattractions.nz/sandfly-bay/ (Accessed: 28th December 2021)

Beddall, L. (2018) Go sandboarding in New Zealand's Northland. Retrieved from The Star: https://www.thestar.com/life/travel/2018/01/08/go-sandboarding-in-new-zealands-northland.html (Accessed: 28th December 2021)

Williams, C. (2019) Tourist dies at Te Paki Sand Dunes after being run over by bus. Retrieved from Stuff: https://www.stuff.co.nz/national/110381458/tourist-dies-at-te-paki-sand-dunes-after-being-run-over-by-bus (Accessed: 28th December 2021)

Rove.me (2019) Sandboarding in Sigatoka. Retrieved from Rove.me: https://rove.me/to/fiji/sigatoka-sandboarding (Accessed: 29th December 2021)

Volcano Discovery (n.d.) Yasur Volcano. Retrieved from Volcano Discovery: https://www.volcanodiscovery.com/yasur.html (Accessed: 29th December 2021)

Istvan, Z. (2002) EXTREME SPORTS / Really Good Pumice, Dude! / Volcano boarding: Russian roulette on a snowboard. Retrieved from SFGATE: https://www.sfgate.com/sports/article/EXTREME-SPORTS-Really-Good-Pumice-Dude-2747600.php (Accessed: 29th December 2021)

www.ingramcontent.com/pod-product-compliance
Lightning Source LLC
Chambersburg PA
CBHW050232120526
44590CB00016B/2054